	DATE DUE		

The Thirteenth Amendment

Other titles in *The Constitution:*

The First Amendment
Freedom of Speech, Religion, and the Press
ISBN: 0-89490-897-9

The Second Amendment
The Right to Own Guns
ISBN:0-89490-925-8

The Fourth Amendment
Search and Seizure
ISBN: 0-89490-924-X

The Fifth Amendment
The Right to Remain Silent
ISBN: 0-89490-894-4

The Thirteenth Amendment
Ending Slavery
ISBN: 0-89490-923-1

The Fifteenth Amendment
African-American Men's Right to Vote
ISBN: 0-7660-1033-3

The Eighteenth and Twenty-First Amendments
Alcohol—Prohibition and Repeal
ISBN: 0-89490-926-6

The Nineteenth Amendment
Women's Right to Vote
ISBN: 0-89490-922-3

The Thirteenth Amendment

Ending Slavery

The
Constitution

Elizabeth Schleichert

Enslow Publishers, Inc.

40 Industrial Road   PO Box 38
Box 398   Aldershot
Berkeley Heights, NJ 07922   Hants GU12 6BP
USA   UK

http://www.enslow.com

Library of Congress Cataloging-in-Publication Data

Schleichert, Elizabeth.
    The Thirteenth Amendment: ending slavery / Elizabeth Schleichert.
        p. cm. — (The Constitution)
    Includes bibliographical references and index.
    Summary: Presents an overview of the history of slavery in the United States, its abolition by constitutional amendment in 1865, and the Reconstruction and its aftermath.
    ISBN 0-89490-923-1
    1. Slavery—Law and legislation—United States—Juvenile literature. 2. Constitutional amendments—United States—13th—Juvenile literature. 3. United States. Constitution. 13th Amendment—History—Juvenile literature. 4. Constitutional amendments—United States. [1. United States. Constitution. 13th Amendment—History. 2. Constitutional amendments. 3. Slavery. 4. Afro-Americans—History.] I. Title. II. Series: Constitution (Springfield, Union County, N.J.)
KF4545.S5S35   1998
342.73'087—DC21   97-34082
                                                              CIP
                                                               AC

Printed in the United States of America.

10 9 8 7 6 5

Photo Credits: New York World-Telegram and Sun Collection, Library of Congress, pp. 89, 95; Reproduced from the collections of the Library of Congress, pp. 9, 17, 27, 29, 37, 42, 49, 54, 64, 70, 76, 83.

Cover Photo: Reproduced from the collections of the Library of Congress

Contents

Nat Turner's Rebellion

It was a steamy, sweltering Sunday evening on August 21, 1831. As dark descended, seven African-American slaves emerged from the woods at Cabin Pond in Southampton County, in the southwestern corner of Virginia. Making their way through the tangle of cypress trees and water oaks, they moved quietly toward a nearby home. It belonged to slaveowner Joseph Travis. The house was dark and still, as Travis, his wife, his son, and a white servant slept soundly. Outside, one of the slaves quietly placed a ladder against the house, near a second floor window. He climbed the ladder, gently opened the window, crawled in, and crept downstairs to the front door. Unbarring the door, he let the others in. All seven quietly sneaked upstairs. A moment later they came back down, grabbed four guns and a few old muskets, and fled to the nearby barn. Not a sound came from above. The household was quiet. All four white members of the household had been axed to death in their sleep.

Once inside the safety of the barn, Nat Turner, the

group's leader, called the men to order. A strikingly
handsome man, with a powerful build and deep-set,
penetrating eyes, the thirty-year-old Turner com-
manded respect.[1] He was a highly intelligent and
deeply religious man, who prayed and fasted often and
who sensed God had called him to a special mission.[2]
For some time now, Turner had been preaching fiery
sermons to the slaves on Sundays. He kept them spell-
bound with his charismatic voice and his dreams of
liberation for himself and other slaves. Nat Turner was
on fire with a deep rage over the injustice of slavery, of
being treated as a piece of property, bought and sold,
whipped and punished, fed scraps and worked cease-
lessly. His anger was matched by his faith and a
burning sense of mission. Nat Turner felt himself a
rebel in God's service.[3] As he himself told it, he had
seen a vision of "white spirits and black spirits
engaged in a battle."[4] He had also heard a voice from
heaven, saying "I should arise and prepare myself, and
slay my enemies with their own weapons."[5]

His plan was simple, if not fully formed: He and
his men would attack the area slaveholders, house by
house, picking up slaves, weapons, and horses from
each estate. They would slowly make their way to
Jerusalem, the county seat of Southampton, where
they would find enough ammunition to take control of
all of Southampton County. Beyond that, the plan was
vague. Apparently, Nat Turner expected God to guide
him once his rebellion was launched.[6] Perhaps he and
his band would end up in the Dismal Swamp, a huge,
murky haven, long used as a hideout by fugitive slaves.
Presumably, once there he might set up headquarters
from which to raid slaveholding centers in Virginia
and North Carolina.[7]

Whatever Turner's ultimate aim, in order for his

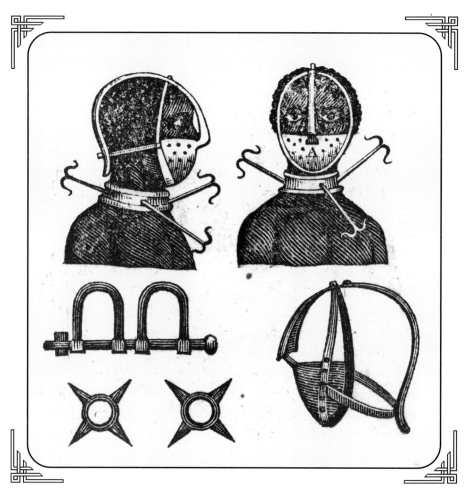

This woodcut from the 1807 book The Penitential Tyrant, by Thomas Branigan, shows an iron mask, collar, leg shackles, and spurs that were used to restrain slaves. This type of cruel treatment inspired Nat Turner to lead a violent rebellion of slaves against their masters.

initial ten-mile sweep to Jerusalem to succeed, swift attack and secrecy were critical. He ordered his men to leave no white person alive. He wanted to inspire fear and alarm among his enemies.[8] Eventually, he would spare women and children, and those who did not resist. He claimed to be leading a struggle for liberty.

Once the Travis attack was over, Turner instructed his small band of followers in the barn on the use of their newly acquired weapons until he was satisfied that his men could handle the guns. Then, he led them back out into the night. Keeping to the shadows, the group proceeded, unnoticed, down the road until they came to the next slaveholder's home. There, they went to work again. House by house, the scene was repeated in quick succession. Within twenty-four hours sixty whites had been killed. The word spread like wildfire through the neighboring slave community that Nat Turner was on the march, and his small band soon swelled to seventy followers.

Turner was determined to destroy what he could of the system that had enslaved and humiliated his people for years. He and his men headed on toward Jerusalem, leaving the white community seemingly paralyzed for miles around. But just outside Jerusalem, against Nat Turner's advice, a few of his men stopped at a plantation to recruit more slaves. Some of them went inside the house, while the others waited by the gate. With their group divided, they were vulnerable. Suddenly, out of nowhere, two patrols of white men descended, forcing Turner's men to fight on two fronts. The stolen weapons proved inadequate, and Turner and his men were soon overpowered. A few were captured, while others were killed or wounded. The rest scattered and were eventually caught. Nat Turner escaped. He was cut off from his men and found himself alone.

Meantime, a force of about three thousand white men from Virginia and North Carolina were converging on Southampton to put down the slave revolt.

Turner later described how he "scratched a hole under a pile of fence rails in a field," not far from the Travis house, where, "I concealed myself for six weeks, never leaving my hiding place but for a few minutes in the dead of night to get water, which was very near."[9] A reward was out on his head, and he was widely sought. He did not know that in the days following his revolt, slaves and free blacks who were innocent of any part in his rebellion were massacred. One newspaper stated: "Men were tortured to death, burned, maimed and subjected to nameless atrocities. The overseers were called upon to point out any slaves whom they distrusted, and if any tried to escape they were cut down."[10] More than one hundred African Americans were murdered in Southampton County in retaliation for Turner's misdeeds. The killings went on for a full year.

Meantime, Nat Turner continued to hide. He was fulfilling a dream that had been long in the making. It was unimaginable that he would admit defeat. He felt it was his destiny to be a leader of his people. He was born a slave in Southampton County, Virginia, in 1800. He had been just three or four years old when his mother overheard him telling other children about an event that had taken place before he had been born. She tried to point out to him that he could not know about these things, since he had not been alive at the time. But he insisted he knew all about it. Later, Nat recalled, "I surely would be a prophet, as the Lord had shewn [sic] me things that had happened before my birth."[11]

Nat Turner was different from most other young slaves in other ways, too. He learned how to read and write (both were forbidden by slave laws) and always tried to improve his mind. He became extremely religious and spent a great deal of time praying and reading his Bible. He also preached. While working in the fields, he said he heard voices, which told him of just one thing—freedom.[12] It was in 1825 when Turner's vision of white and black spirits fighting called him to action. In his vision "the thunder rolled in the Heavens, and blood flowed in streams."[13] A voice, he said, told him that he would see such things and that he should look for signs in the heavens, about when he should be prepared to begin the fight. The sign for action, according to Turner, was the eclipse of the sun in February 1831. Immediately, Nat called together a few other slaves and began to meet regularly with them to discuss a slave rebellion.

As Nat Turner continued to hide near the Travis place in his dugout cave under the fence rails, a dog forced him out. The animal had been attracted to the spot by some meat Turner had hidden. Two hunters followed the dog there. When they saw Turner emerge from the spot, the two men ran. But Turner knew that he was no longer safe in his cave.

For two more weeks he was on the run, constantly evading capture. Men swarmed all over the woods and swamps, hot on his trail, dreaming of winning the $1,000 reward out on him. Finally, on October 30, as Turner poked his head out of yet another hiding spot under a fallen tree, he confronted a man whose gun was aimed right at his head. The man told Turner to surrender or else he would be shot. So ended Turner's two months of running and his dream of freedom.

The next day, the half-starved, bone-thin escapee was hauled into court in Jerusalem, Virginia, for questioning. He admitted that he alone had been the one to start and direct the killing of the white people. He refused to confess, however, that he had done any wrong. In fact, he declared that if he could do it again, "he must necessarily act in the same way."[14] Soon afterward, he was condemned to death by hanging.

On November 11, around noon, the sheriff led Nat Turner out to a gnarled tree just to the northeast of Jerusalem. A huge crowd was gathered. The sheriff asked Nat if he had anything to say before he died. He simply replied that he was ready. At that, he went calmly to his death, and as the rope attached to the noose was suspended from the old tree, he stirred not even a muscle. Nat Turner's rebellion and death marked a turning point in the history of slavery.

He also left a lasting legacy among African Americans, to whom he was a hero. Slaves and their descendants upheld his name as a legend. Among many of them, Nat Turner's rebellion became known as the "first war" against slavery, and the Civil War eventually was the second. Turner was enshrined as a martyr in the cause of freedom.

2

The Constitution and Slavery

In the summer of 1787, forty-four years before Nat Turner staged his rebellion, fifty-five men were hard at work in an elegant chamber in the State House (now called Independence Hall) off Chestnut Street in Philadelphia. They were debating, arguing, and crafting the provisions of a lengthy document, called the Constitution. This gathering, called the Constitutional Convention, included America's most distinguished citizens: George Washington, James Madison, Benjamin Franklin, Alexander Hamilton, and others. Many had fought in the American Revolution and had signed the Declaration of Independence in this very same building.

George Washington had led the Continental army to victory in the Revolution. Serving as deputy from Virginia, Washington was elected the convention's president when it first convened in late May. He accepted this honor with his usual modesty. He said that he had few qualifications for the job and that he hoped any mistakes he might make would be forgiven.[1] Washington kept himself apart from the debates and emotional arguments that would erupt over the next four months. But the power of his quiet presence held the convention together and kept the proceedings going.

The eighty-one-year-old Ben Franklin—inventor, peacemaker, diplomat, essayist—rivaled Washington as elder statesman. He was by now rather feeble, but he still had great charm and a fine sense of humor. He would help to smooth over disputes when tempers flared.[2]

In this steamy Philadelphia summer, Washington, Franklin, and the other delegates were facing one of the biggest challenges of their careers: How to reinvent the nation's government before the country fell apart. Since the end of the American Revolution in 1782, the United States had been loosely run by a Congress. No one person, such as a president was in charge. America had won the Revolution and escaped the tyranny of the British king. Americans had gone on to deliberately establish a central or federal government that had little power. But by now, it was clear to the delegates in Philadelphia that this governmental system, established by a document known as the Articles of Confederation, was ineffective. Congress was unable to enforce laws or collect taxes. The states were acting like independent nations, not like a union of equals. They were fighting with each other over all sorts of things, such as boundaries and commerce routes. Rebellions broke out here and there. It seemed that we could win a difficult war like the American Revolution against a common enemy (the British) but that we could not keep order among ourselves.

Uncertain of how to proceed, the delegates knew they had to reinvent a stronger central government for

The back of the State House in Philadelphia is shown in an 1800 engraving by William Birch and Son. Now known as Independence Hall, the State House was the location for the Constitutional Convention.

the sake of preserving their United States. All summer they gave it their best effort. Taking their seats, the men (there were no women) arranged themselves three or four to a table. Then they got to work, debating and arguing, writing and rewriting, proposing and re-proposing the clauses and provisions of the new document they were creating. Seldom has a group of people wrestled with the fine points of democratic government with such passion and care as did the members of the Constitutional Convention. The delib-erations of the convention were to be conducted in secret. To ensure this, armed guards were posted around the State House. And to further encourage the delegates to focus without outside interruptions, loose dirt was spread on the surrounding streets to quiet the sounds of passing horses, wagons, and carriages.[3]

One issue kept threatening to destroy the conven-tion's work—the existence of slavery in the United States. Typical of those who opposed it was the thirty-five-year-old delegate from New York, Gouverneur Morris. Morris was recognizable by his wooden leg, the result of a horse-driving accident. Clutching his cane, stomping awkwardly to a standing position, he glanced around at his fellow delegates with flashing eyes and launched into a blunt attack on slavery. Calling it a curse, he urged his fellow delegates to travel through the whole country and note the difference between the fine culture of the free, nonslave regions and the "misery and poverty" that is common in the slave states.[4]

Morris chose to ignore the fact that his state of New York at the time still had twenty thousand slaves.[5] But in fairness, while slavery still existed in some northern states, over the past few years since the American Revolution, northern lawmakers had begun taking steps to make it illegal. As a result, slavery was slowly becoming confined to the South. In 1787 there were more than seven hundred thousand slaves in this country, more than one sixth of the population.[6] Hundreds of thousands of men, women, and children toiled in the cotton, rice, indigo, and tobacco fields of the South, with little hope of ever seeing freedom. Many freethinking, moral white southerners, such as George Washington and Thomas Jefferson, had slaves but disliked slavery as a blight on the free republic. They hoped that slavery would somehow die of its own accord.[7] However, at the convention, delegates from the deep South, led by those from South Carolina and Georgia, ardently defended slavery. They threatened to walk away from the proceedings if slavery were not protected by the new Constitution.

Slavery became an issue in connection with the most hotly debated subject at the convention: namely, how the states should be represented in Congress. The small states felt each of them should have an equal vote. Eventually, the Senate, the upper lawmaking body in Congress, was established in this way, with each state having two senators. Then debate centered around the House of Representatives, the lower lawmaking body in Congress. Its elected members would be based on some other formula. The large states, for obvious reasons, felt the number should be based on the population of each state. In figuring population, the South wanted slaves included as full persons in this count. The North did not want slaves to be considered at all in the count. For three weeks this issue was debated. Elbridge Gerry of Massachusetts demanded to know why the North could not count its animals in tallying its representatives if the South could include slaves. He said that if slaves were to be counted as property, then so should the property of the North—namely, horses and cattle.[8]

After much wrangling, James Wilson of the Pennsylvania delegation put forth a compromise. Scottish born, and speaking with a heavy burr, Wilson suggested that the number of representatives from each state in the House be based on the number of free citizens as well as "three fifths of everyone else except Indians."[9] The three fifths referred to slaves. In other words, five slaves would be counted as equal to three other people. This represented a compromise for both southerners and northerners. Eventually, Wilson's proposal was accepted. Slavery, then, was acknowledged in the Constitution, without actually being named as such.

It reared its head yet again when the delegates were hammering out the role of Congress in the area of trade and commerce. A question arose about the slave trade. Should the states or the Congress control it or should it be abolished? Charles Pinckney of South Carolina stated his viewpoint clearly. He said that South Carolina would never agree to any government that prohibited the slave trade. Besides, Pinckney said, by way of justifying slavery, "In all ages, one half of mankind have been slaves."[10] And he said, perhaps as a way to calm his critics, that if left alone, the southern states would eventually stop importing slaves. Fearing to lose the support of the southern delegates, another compromise was written into the Constitution. The importation of slaves would be legal until 1808 after which it would be forbidden. Again, the word slave was not used: "The Migration or Importation of such Persons as any of the States now existing shall think proper to admit, shall not be prohibited by the

Congress prior to the year one thousand eight hundred and eight."[11]

In a final deal—one that has since been repeatedly called immoral—favoring the South, a so-called fugitive slave clause was added to the Constitution. "No Person held to Service or Labour in one State, under the Laws thereof, escaping into another, shall . . . be discharged from such Service . . . but shall be delivered up on Claim of the Party to whom such Service or Labour may be due."[12] The word slave or slavery again was not mentioned. But the "Person[s] held to Service or Labour in one State" referred to a slave. And this clause committed the whole country to the return of runaway slaves to their owners. It was yet another sign of the power of slave owners over these proceedings.

The delegates to the convention have since been criticized for not fighting to end slavery then and there. Nat Turner would not have reached the intolerable need to rebel after so many years in bondage if the Constitution had simply banned slavery. Later critics, in fact, called the Constitution a "covenant with death" for its compromises with the slave owners' South.[13] Where was the courage and the nerve of those who knew in their hearts that slavery was wrong? Perhaps there is no way to justify the choices made by the creators of the Constitution, the highest law of our country. But we can try at least to understand their thinking. They were practical men. They had come together to create a more workable kind of government for the United States. Theirs was an extremely sensitive, fragile task. All the states represented at the convention had either until very recently, or still, used slaves, and all claimed to be "sovereign" or independent of one another. All the great names behind the writing of the Constitution morally opposed slavery. But at the same time they understood how important slavery was to the states of the deep South. The choice in the delegates' minds was whether to fight against slavery and lose the chance at creating a workable union of all the states or compromise in order to preserve it.[14] As James Madison wrote to his friend Thomas Jefferson, who was in Paris: "South Carolina and Georgia were inflexible on the point of slaves."[15] Still, delegates such as Madison were weak in the face of this inflexibility, backing down where they could have stood their ground and fought.[16]

For many lawmakers, slavery was a complicated issue. Even some people who detested slavery still depended on it. James Madison, for instance, had grown up on a Virginia plantation where, as a boy, he had played with his family's slaves. Furthermore, he had brought his personal slave with him to Philadelphia. (To his credit, he sold the slave in Philadelphia with the understanding that the man would be freed soon in Pennsylvania.) How could someone with this background condemn slavery? But by choosing to compromise on the slavery question at the Constitutional Convention, the northern delegates bought a United States, as some have said, "at the cost of the rights and freedoms of the Africans and African Americans" in the South.[17] Only after a bloody Civil War was slavery finally ended with the passage of the Thirteenth Amendment.

However, today we are still working on issues of equality and at dealing with racial prejudice rooted in slavery. In 1787, the ultimate goal, the framing of a new United States government, took precedence over the issue of slavery. The delegates left it for future generations to deal with. This was unfortunate and ultimately tragic. In fact, the silent acceptance of slavery in the Constitution was the first seed that would lead to disunion and to the Civil War in fewer than one hundred years.

While this was a drastic mistake, much of what the delegates to the convention achieved by September 1787 was noteworthy. They had invented perhaps the most complex type of government ever. It was a strong, democratic, centralized system with three branches: an elected executive, the president; an elected law-making body, Congress; and a judicial branch, the Supreme Court. Each branch of the government was given limited power, with each balancing, or offsetting, the others. Article V of the Constitution allowed for a process by which new national laws, called amendments, could be added to the Constitution.

The delegates signed the completed Constitution on September 17, 1787. On September 28, Congress sent it to the states for approval. According to the Constitution itself, nine states (a two-thirds majority) had to ratify, or approve it, before it would become the law of the land. By late June 1788, the ninth state, New Hampshire, had done so.

For all its initial flaws, our Constitution has endured longer—more than two hundred years—than any other modern written constitution.[18] Today, as the ultimate law of the land, it continues to bind all fifty states.

A Historical Overview of Slavery

The first Africans to come to North America—a mere twenty of them—were put ashore at Jamestown, Virginia, in 1619. They were probably off-loaded by pirates who had stolen their slave cargo on the high seas. For a time, there were few others. The colonists were slow to adopt the institution of slavery. Instead, they relied on indentured servants, mostly Englishmen, to work the land and do other menial jobs for them. The servants got free passage over. For this, they agreed to work for four to seven years under a master. While they were treated as slaves, they did have the chance to become free men and women. So long as there was a ready supply of indentured servants the colonists saw no point in going to the trouble of importing Africans. After all, they did not speak the language and required a long period of adjustment to the culture. But from the 1680s on, things changed. More and more African slaves arrived here. For example, between 1680 and 1750, the African-American population in Virginia increased from 7 percent to 44 percent.[1] Many factors affected this change. In England wages rose and more jobs were available. With these improved conditions, fewer white laborers felt the need to try their luck as indentured servants in the colonies. The colonists turned instead to African slaves, who could be obtained more cheaply than white indentured servants.

Those who were shipped to the New World were the strongest, most talented, and cultured of West Africa's young men and women. Rounded up in their homeland, chained, and marched overland to a coastal slave-trading port, the victims were terrified. Many had never before seen the ocean, ships, or white men. "I was now persuaded that I had gotten into a world of bad spirits and that they were going to kill me," wrote Olaudah Equiano, a slave who endured this experience.[2]

The voyage across the ocean to the New World, which could last three months, was nearly unbearable. Still chained together, the slaves were crammed into the filthy hold of ships in a space so small that they could hardly turn over. Smallpox killed many, as did other diseases caused by overcrowding and unsanitary conditions. Unable to stand and barely able to move, the slaves suffered terribly. An eleven-year-old boy, Gustavus Vassa, was captured in Dahomey (now Benin) in West Africa in 1756. He later wrote about the voyage: "I became so sick and low that I was not able to eat, nor had I the least desire to taste anything."[3] The white men on board the ship did not want young Gustavus to starve to death; he would not be worth any money to them if he died. So when he repeatedly refused to eat, they took him on deck, laid him across the windlass (a barrel-shaped crank for hoisting the sails), and whipped him. Other forms of punishment

The first African slaves arrive at Jamestown, Virginia, in 1619. Twenty slaves were carried on this ship and later sold in North America, as depicted in this 1901 painting in Harper's magazine.

were doled out to slaves who refused food or showed other signs of rebellion. To escape their suffering, many leaped overboard and drowned themselves.

Those who survived the cruelties of the journey faced a grim future. Most were sold into slavery in Brazil or in the islands of the Caribbean. The rest ended up in the American colonies, soon to be called the United States. Though the importation of slaves was banned in 1808, the United States, by then, had acquired enough to make for a sizable population. By the year 1810, there were more than 1 million slaves in the United States, and their numbers more than tripled again to almost 4 million in 1860.[4]

Slavery became especially entrenched in regions where there was large-scale agriculture, which depended on a sizable number of laborers to work the fields. This included much of the South. By 1860 slaves worked on cotton, tobacco, hemp, sugar, and rice farms and plantations in fourteen southern states. A critical development further ensured slavery's hold on the South: In 1793 the cotton gin was invented. It mechanically separated the fleecy cotton fibers from their seeds. This process had once taken a single slave ten hours to pull the seeds from only one pound of cotton. Now, the cotton gin could process one thousand pounds a day. As a result, cotton became a profitable crop. It was turned into cloth both in the United States and overseas, especially in England. The demand for more slaves to pick cotton in the lower South increased. Southerners bought more and more slaves.

No matter their position, or circumstances, most slaves were completely dependent on their masters, who generally expected them to work as hard as possible.[5] From about the age of twelve, slaves toiled twelve to fifteen hours a day, in all kinds of weather. Overwork

A white overseer with a whip directs a group of slaves in an engraving from the 1862 book South Carolina and the Ex-Slaves *by A. M. French.*

was constant. Picking cotton was tough, painful work. The thorny casing of the cotton cut the fingers, and the feet and backs of the slaves ached from the bending over and plodding up and down the long rows of cotton in the hot sun. Solomon Northrup described how the cotton workers had to be in the field at first light in the morning and were given only a ten- to fifteen-minute lunch break to eat cold bacon.[6] They were not allowed a minute's rest until nightfall.

The aim of plantation management was outlined in 1833 by a South Carolina planter. "The slave should know that his master is to govern absolutely, that he is to obey implicitly."[7] The slave always had to be kept submissive and under the master's absolute authority. Masters made sure that their charges knew that misbehavior might result in some form of brutal punishment. This was the master's way of maintaining power and control over his slaves. The most common disciplinary measure was a whipping. It was done using a long rawhide whip, which tore the skin from the back. Standard whippings were fifteen to twenty lashes, though serious offenses required hundreds.[8]

Some masters took a personal interest in the lives of their slaves, knew them by name, and frequently talked with them, supervising their work and also looking after their welfare. The slaves were treated as inferior members of the household. Some fed and clothed their slaves reasonably well and granted them considerable freedom to marry, have private garden plots, and enjoy religious and social gatherings.

But most slaves lived a life of deprivation and poverty. Their food was poor—a little bit of corn and salt pork or bacon. This was occasionally supplemented by sweet potatoes, peas, rice, syrup, and fruit. A slave's clothing was made of a shabby, rough material that scratched the skin. Many went barefoot. Either their shoes were worn out or did not fit, or they never received any at all. Slaves were crowded into small one-room shacks with dirt floors, leaky roofs, and drafty walls. When it rained, the floor got wet and muddy. Diseases abounded. Malaria, yellow fever, typhoid, tetanus, and pneumonia killed many at an early age. Fewer than four out of one hundred slaves lived sixty years or more.[9]

The separating of families was one of the cruelest aspects of slavery. Marriages among slaves had no legal basis. Masters might desire to keep families together, but often economic necessity overrode other considerations. Inevitably, husbands and wives, parents and children were separated. Should a slave desire to leave home to visit other family members, he or she needed a master's permission. A written pass or white escort was necessary to leave the plantation. Sometimes, permission was denied. Many slaves simply ran off, either to find family members or to get away from a cruel master. Advertisements for runaway slaves in many southern papers testify to the frequency of this practice as slaves sought to be reunited with loved ones.

From the *Richmond* (Va.) *Enquirer*, February 20, 1838.

$10 REWARD FOR A NEGRO WOMAN, NAMED SALLY, 40 YEARS OLD. WE HAVE JUST REASON TO BELIEVE THE SAID NEGRO TO BE NOW LURKING ON THE JAMES RIVER CANAL, OR IN THE GREEN SPRING NEIGHBORHOOD, WHERE, WE ARE INFORMED, HER HUSBAND RESIDES. THE ABOVE REWARD WILL BE GIVEN TO ANY PERSON SECURING HER.[10]

Polly C. Shields

Mount Elba, February 19, 1838.

From the *Macon* (Ga.) *Messenger*, January 16, 1839.

RAN AWAY FROM THE SUBSCRIBER, TWO SLAVES, DAVIS, A MAN ABOUT 45 YEARS OLD; ALSO PEGGY, HIS WIFE, NEAR THE SAME AGE. SAID NEGROES WILL PROBABLY MAKE THEIR WAY TO COLUMBIA COUNTY, AS THEY HAVE CHILDREN LIVING IN THAT COUNTY. I WILL LIBERALLY REWARD ANY PERSON WHO MAY DELIVER THEM TO ME.[11]

Nehemiah King

The basic freedoms whites took for granted were denied to slaves. Slaves had no rights or privileges. Most were not allowed to own any property or have any money, so they could not buy anything. They had no books or schools. They could not gather together unless a white adult was present. They could not choose what kind of work to do or where they wanted to live. They could not go into town when they felt like it or rest when they were tired.

Slaves early on showed resentment against their status and treatment. In eighteenth-century Virginia, for instance, there were several cases of slave cooks poisoning their owners.[12] In 1739 slaves near Charleston, South Carolina, killed two guards in a warehouse and stole guns.[13] For several days they went on a rampage, killing whites and attempting to put an end to slavery in that area. A century later Nat Turner followed suit, only to end up hanging from a tree. More than one hundred other slaves, many innocent, were killed for suspected participation in his, or other, revolts. Sometimes slaves rebelled in less obvious ways. They might slow up their work pace, pretend to be sick, or act as if they did not understand a job. Some would lose or damage tools or start fires.[14] Despite the fact that meetings were forbidden, slaves would manage to gather together, swap stories, and sing songs that held the promise of a new freedom. Many of the words used biblical themes to express this yearning:

> *Didn't my Lord deliver Daniel,*
> *deliver Daniel, deliver Daniel?*
> *Didn't my Lord deliver Daniel,*
> *Then why not every man?*[15]

The Seeds of Disunion and Civil War

4

In 1861 British newspaper reporter William Howard Russell visited the United States. When his steamship docked in New York Harbor, he noticed a great deal of activity, with ferryboats and freighters easing in and out of the port. Beyond, he could see the towering factories where railroad parts, metal goods, and machinery were made. On the bustling docks as he disembarked, Russell rubbed shoulders with throngs of immigrants, who spoke in many different foreign languages.[1]

Much of northern industry was built on immigrant labor. From 1831 to 1860, nearly 5 million immigrants from Europe flocked to the United States.[2] They came for different reasons: Many were seeking jobs and cheap land or escaping famine and grinding poverty. Others were fleeing political or religious tyranny and oppression. Most settled in the Northeast or moved to the newly settled West. Relatively few went south. In the North, they provided a cheap source of labor for the rapidly expanding factories. Industrial managers preferred hiring immigrants to slaves. Immigrants could be hired and fired at will. Also, a slave-based agriculture was not needed here because there were few large farms in the North. In fact, ever since the late 1700s, the northern states, one by one, had abolished slavery.

When William Howard Russell traveled south by train, he was struck by how different this region was from the North.[3] Instead of large manufacturing centers, he found farmlands stretching for miles. The largest farms, or plantations, grew a single crop, such as tobacco, rice, sugarcane, or cotton. They relied on slaves to work the fields. The biggest city Russell visited was New Orleans. It seemed small compared with the urban centers of the North he had left behind. Here everywhere he went were signs of slavery. Many cities had auction blocks where African Americans were displayed for sale. At slave sales, buyers would pry open the slave's mouth to look at teeth, as though the merchandise was cattle.[4]

In the South, Russell encountered very different attitudes from those in the North. Southerners complained of their northern neighbors' greed. The North bought the bales of cotton from their fields for what planters considered too low a price. Then they shipped much of it overseas for too high a fee, according to southern critics. The rest of the cotton was processed into cloth in northern mill towns. Southern planters had no choice: they had to buy their cloth from northerners or from England, relying on northern ships and northern middlemen to get it to them. Not just cotton, but other necessary manufactured goods all came from northern factories. The South became more resentful and fearful of the North as it grew in wealth and economic prosperity.[5] In 1851 a newspaper in Alabama

This 1862 photo by Timothy O'Sullivan shows slaves preparing cotton to be put through the gin. After the cotton was refined, it was sold and shipped to the northern states, where it was processed in the industrial centers and sold.

noted all the ways in which the South was dependent on the North:

> We purchase all our luxuries and necessities from the North. Our slaves work with Northern hoes and plows. The slave owner dresses in Northern goods, rides in a Northern saddle. In Northern vessels his products are carried to market, his cotton is ginned with Northern gins. His son is educated at a Northern college.[6]

Some observers believed that the North and the South were practically two separate nations, which were united only by their dislike of each other.[7]

The existence of slavery in the South sharpened the divide between the two regions. During the early 1800s more and more northerners opposed the existence of slavery. They became known as abolitionists. They wanted to see an end to slavery. Southerners became defensive and developed arguments justifying slavery. "I believe our slaves are the happiest three millions of human beings on whom the sun shines," wrote South Carolina plantation owner and governor, James Henry Hammond.[8] Southern leaders said northerners were exaggerating the evils of slavery. They questioned the right of the North to interfere in their affairs.[9] Instead, they made slave laws tighter and tighter as time went by.

As the West began to be settled, the slavery issue became more heated. A series of political crises sharpened the tension between the North and the South. In the 1800s many Americans had headed to the western frontier, hoping to make a fortune farming cheap, fertile land. Before 1812 the frontier lay just beyond the Appalachians. It was not long before pioneers pressed this line of settlement westward. For instance, many Georgia and North and South Carolina farmers and planters at the southern end of the

Appalachians headed west to the Missouri Territory to find fertile soil for cotton farming. Some planters, who followed the first wave of small farmers, traveled in style. The dusty and muddy roads bore whole caravans of their goods piled on carts and wagons and pack horses. Herds of cattle and sheep stretched out for miles, as did long lines of slaves. At the rear rode the planter and his family in carriages. Soon, frontiersmen in the Missouri Territory applied to Congress to make their region the twenty-third state in the Union. (According to the law, when the population of any western territory reached sixty thousand, the people living there could apply to Congress to be admitted to the Union as a state.)

By 1819, as Congress considered this measure, there were already about ten thousand slaves in Missouri, making up a sixth of the total population.[10] If Missouri were admitted to the Union, therefore, it would be a proslavery state. This alarmed many northerners. Out of the twenty-two states making up the United States, eleven were slave states (states in which slavery was permitted) and eleven were free, or nonslave states. As a result, each section had an equal vote in Congress. If Missouri joined the Union as a slave state, it would give the South more political power. For this reason, the North opposed Missouri's becoming a slave state. Southerners feared that unless their slave-based cotton agriculture was allowed to expand westward, their entire economy would die. Farming in the already populated regions of the South was becoming more difficult. This was because the soil was wearing out or being washed away in heavy rains. Westward expansion was necessary to preserve the southern way of life, so the argument went.

Thanks to Congressman Henry Clay from

Kentucky, a compromise was reached. Clay was a master at bringing together people of opposing viewpoints and getting them to agree on a solution. He did this partly by making lively speeches in Congress that made fun of each side. He was also quite a showman. One of the highlights of a Clay speech was his springing up from a crouch to his full six feet to make a point at a particularly dramatic moment.[11] Clay proposed that Missouri be admitted as a slave state. To balance it, Maine, which had just broken off from Massachusetts, could be admitted as a free state. He suggested that a line be drawn across the remaining unsettled territory defining where slavery would and would not be permitted in the future. Finally, in 1820, Congress agreed to his solution. This marked the first time that a law passed by Congress set one section of the country against another. For nearly thirty years, this Missouri Compromise helped keep the country intact. But some sensed that more trouble lay ahead. Thomas Jefferson wrote: "This momentous question, like a fire bell in the night, awakened and filled me with terror."[12] John Quincy Adams, who in another decade would become president, wrote in his diary: "I take it for granted that the present question is a mere preamble—a title-page to a great, tragic volume."[13]

In fact, it was almost thirty years after the Missouri Compromise before another political crisis sparked the old sectional rivalries. In 1846, the United States went to war with Mexico. Two years later, the United States won. As a result of this victory, the United States acquired nearly 1 million square miles of new territory in the Southwest, extending from Texas to the Pacific Coast. Instead of rejoicing over this, politicians began fighting over the future of the new land even before the war was won. David Wilmot, a tobacco-chewing country lawyer and congressman from Pennsylvania, introduced a bill into Congress. In it, he suggested that slavery be prohibited in any of the lands won from Mexico. Wilmot's Proviso, as the bill was called, never became law. It did stir up strong feelings in both the North and the South, however. A southern congressman reflected the feelings of many in his region by asserting that if the North were trying to drive southerners from the territories, then he was for pulling out of the Union.[14]

Disunion (the breaking apart of the United States) was a serious threat. It seemed more real as tensions mounted. Every time southern and northern leaders tried to discuss the proviso, they ended up screaming angrily and yelling insults at each other.

It was Henry Clay, now age seventy-three and ailing, who again stepped in to try to soothe over the conflict. Many of his colleagues had thought him too old or distracted to be much help. During recent angry debates in Congress, they had seen him apparently daydreaming as he munched on peppermint candy or played with his snuffbox. But Clay had, in fact, been thinking up a plan the whole time.

On a cold February morning in 1850, the Kentucky senator took to the floor to make an important speech in the Senate. His rich, deep voice rose out over the floor as ladies in wide hooped skirts rustled in quickly to take their seats in the visitors' section. Clay said that this was too somber a moment for him to make a dramatic performance. Instead, for three hours, he begged his fellow congressmen to use reason and to drop their sectional jealousies for the sake of the Union. He presented his specific suggestions for compromise one by one. He urged southerners to allow California to enter the Union as a free state. In

As seen in this 1850 lithograph, the passage of the Fugitive Slave Law meant that escaped slaves were no longer safe from capture, even in states where slavery was outlawed. The new law increased tensions between the North and the South.

the rest of the new land, he suggested that local settlers decide on their own whether or not to allow slavery. He pleaded with southerners not to pull away from the Union. He expressed hope that if disunion should ever happen, he would not be alive to witness it.

Clay's suggestions were adopted. Other minor resolutions were agreed to as part of this so-called Compromise of 1850. One, aimed at making the South happy, would soon prove troublesome. It was called the Fugitive Slave Law. It allowed the federal government to recapture runaway slaves and return them to their masters. In fact, relatively few slaves attempted to escape. Perhaps only a thousand got away every year.[15] But with the passage of this law, professional slave hunters now charged northward, hoping to stalk down escapees. Sometimes they even kidnapped free former slaves. This infuriated many northerners. Even those who had once been ignorant or indifferent toward slavery became angry. Blacks and whites in northern cities formed vigilance committees to protect fugitives from slave catchers. Abolitionism became more popular. Some ministers preached civil disobedience, urging their parishioners not to cooperate with slave-catching authorities.

So at midcentury the Union seemed threatened by severe division. The possibility of future understanding between the North and the South further dimmed when Henry Clay died two years after the passage of the Compromise of 1850. The rumble of war seemed not that far distant.

Harriet Tubman's Story

In 1849, while the politicians in Washington, D.C., were still debating the resolutions of the Compromise of 1850, slavery continued unabated throughout the South. On a farm near Cambridge, Maryland, a twenty-nine-year-old female slave rose early every morning to trudge off to the fields where she hoed, plowed, and carted produce. Her name was Harriet Tubman and she was married to a freed slave named John. Tubman's parents, themselves slaves, lived nearby, as did many of her brothers and sisters. Her owner frequently hired her out to work on neighboring farms. As a result, Harriet Tubman traveled around the countryside and enjoyed a taste of freedom. Bright and rebellious, she fought against her enslavement. Ever since she had witnessed her two sisters being sold to a slave trader and taken away in chains, she had long feared she would be sold to somebody far away. She dreaded the thought of being torn away from her family against her will. Then, one day, she heard some terrible news. A slave on a nearby plantation told her that a Georgia slave trader was in the area. Apparently, he was going to sell Tubman and her brothers to a plantation farther south, where she would face a worse fate. Many southern plantation slaves toiled for fourteen hours a day in the fields under cruel overseers.

Harriet Tubman had already had her fill of slavery. One of eleven children in her family, she was born into slavery in about 1820 in Bucktown, Maryland. She was named Araminta "Minty" Ross at birth. The young toddler ran barefoot, chasing rabbits and playing near the corn and wheat fields. But at age five her carefree life came to an end. Minty's owner hired her out to nearby white families to earn extra money for himself. She tended babies and cleaned houses. At one point, she became so thin and exhausted that the mistress who had hired her took her back to Minty's owner and said she was not worth any money. Minty's mother nursed her back to health.

Minty remained spunky and tried to outwit the mistresses for whom she was hired out to work. One of them often whipped her in the morning. To keep herself from getting hurt by the whip, Minty learned to put on extra layers of clothing when she got dressed. She also pretended to cry and to fake pain during her beatings. Later in the day, unharmed, she would sneak away and remove the extra clothes. Once when she was caught reaching for a sugar cube, she escaped a whipping by fleeing out the door and jumping into the pigsty. Here she stayed for five days, eating nothing but the scraps that were thrown to the pigs. Near starvation, she finally had to turn herself in and suffer the punishment.

The unrelenting work and brutal punishment were hard on the young girl. Soon Minty, who adopted her mother's name, Harriet, was hired out for tougher jobs, such as cutting down timber and working the fields. She plowed, carted manure, and drove oxen. She built up her physical strength and was able to keep enough of the money she earned as a hired hand to buy herself a pair of oxen worth forty dollars.[1]

As Tubman traveled around, she heard stories. Some were about a strange "Underground Railroad." She learned that this was not any single train or train line, but a series of secret escape routes. People called stationmasters, or agents, would help escaping slaves by hiding them in their homes or taking them to the next secret hiding place, or station stop.

Running away was a huge risk for a slave like Harriet Tubman. If caught, she could suffer any of several punishments: whippings, cropping (cutting off of the ears), or branding with a hot iron.[2] Patrols of local white men with tracking dogs set out to find runaways. If the slave were shot during capture, the killers were never punished. Cash rewards were given to the patrolmen who brought the escapee back.

Harriet Tubman considered her situation carefully. During the past several years she had had a recurring vision. Most often it came upon her when she was returning home after a long day's work in the fields. She would see herself almost flying over fields, towns, and rivers, as though she were a bird. Suddenly, she would be stopped by a river. She would feel herself start to sink. But often just then, a row of women dressed in radiant white gowns would reach out to her, pulling her across the boundary and welcoming her. This vision was always accompanied by voices urging her to run for her life.

Now, facing a grim future, she made up her mind. She said to herself, "There's two things I got a right to and these are Death and Liberty. One or the other I mean to have. No one will take me back alive; I shall fight for my liberty. . . ."[3] Despite the risks, Harriet Tubman resolved to flee. Her husband seemed indifferent to her plan, so she resolved to go alone. She was a strong, capable person. She planned to head north, guided by the North Star and other natural signs, such as the moss that grew thicker on the north side of trees. Years of overhearing whispered conversations about escape routes and strategies came in handy now.

One night, without telling a soul of her plans, Tubman set out. She headed east, along the Greenbriar Swamp into Bucktown. The details about her escape are sketchy. From all accounts, the home of a Quaker woman in Bucktown was her first stop. Here, Harriet was told where to head next and given the name of a sympathizer who would help. She followed these directions and took with her a paper from the Quaker woman, introducing her to the next sympathizer. She had to keep her wits about her, traveling at night, avoiding roads, traveling through wet swamplands, where her tracks and smell would be hidden from pursuing dogs and trackers. She developed an inner sense about when danger threatened and trusted in her God to guide her. She made her way turning northeast along the Choptank River into Delaware. She found help along the Underground Railroad, being directed from one station stop to the next. Many Quakers lived along her route and were happy to hide runaways in their barns, cellars, and attics. Others helped smuggle runaways under the false floors of wagons or ships. The goal was to cross the Mason-Dixon line that separated Delaware from Pennsylvania, which marked the division between slave territory and freedom. Harriet crossed this line early one morning. She later recalled the moment. "I looked at my hands to see if I was the

Dreaming of freedom for herself and other slaves, Harriet Tubman fled from her master and found freedom in the North with the help of the Underground Railroad.

same person. There was such a glory over everything.
The sun came up like gold through the trees, and I felt
like I was in heaven."[4]

Just over the Mason-Dixon line were more abolitionists eager to help fugitive slaves reach
Philadelphia. Having arrived safely, Harriet found a
job as a cook in a hotel. She tried out a variety of
jobs—housekeeper, laundress, cook—taking pleasure
in her freedom to find new work whenever she wanted. Harriet had a plan in mind. She carefully saved her
money. She stashed it away toward the day when she
could bring other slaves, especially her family, north to
freedom. In 1850, a year after her own escape, she
returned south to Baltimore. She would help bring her
half sister, Mary Ann Bowley, and her two children
north to Philadelphia. Mary Ann had narrowly
escaped being sold in Cambridge, Maryland, and with
the help of various Underground Railroad helpers,
had reached Baltimore via boat and wagon and foot.
Harriet met them in a brick house in the city and
helped them reach Philadelphia.

In 1851 Harriet, again risking her life, returned to
Maryland and successfully brought her brother John
to freedom. Soon after this, Harriet went back again.
This time she hoped to persuade her husband, John
Tubman, to join her in Philadelphia. She donned a
man's suit and hat as a disguise and headed back to the
cabin on the old farm that she and John had shared.
She was crushed to discover that John had married
somebody else. He burst out laughing at her sugges-
tion that he come with her. Stung by his rejection,
Harriet Tubman scarcely ever mentioned her husband's name again. She devoted her life from then on
to helping others. On this very trip, when John refused

to go with her, she found ten slaves eager to escape and brought them north.

During these early escape efforts, Harriet Tubman developed many of the techniques she would use in future rescues. She was to make nineteen such excursions, each time risking extreme danger, to bring more than three hundred slaves north.[5] Tubman always plotted a slave escape for a Saturday night. The slaves were often allowed to visit friends on Saturday evening and would not be missed until Monday morning. Notices and rewards posted by the owners alerting people to be on the lookout for missing slaves often would not be printed until Monday or Tuesday. This gave Tubman and her group several nights of travel before being pursued. To further hinder the slave catchers, almost immediately after these notices had been posted on trees and bulletin boards, Tubman's sympathizers would take them all down.

Harriet Tubman always met the escapees eight to ten miles from their plantation. That way, she herself risked fewer chances of being caught. She carried a gun and sharpened stones or clam shells for weapons. She threatened to shoot not just pursuers, but anyone in her group who lost heart and wanted to turn back or be left behind. This was simply her way of preventing betrayal, though she reportedly never actually had to deliver on her threats. At times, Tubman had to go public to make travel arrangements for her fugitives or to beg or scrounge food for the party during the escape. She was talented at assuming different disguises. Sometimes, she dressed well and played the part of an old African-American woman walking down the road. Other times she pretended to be a man. Once when she was walking through a town, she spotted her former master coming toward her. She had with her a pair of live chickens and wore a large sunbonnet over her face. When she saw the danger she was in, she pulled the string attached to the chickens' legs, making them flutter and squawk loudly. As he passed by she bent over, busily tending to the noisy birds.

Key to a successful flight north was absolute silence at times. Tubman always made sure the babies did not cry. She carried them herself in a knapsack around her waist (some accounts say in a basket) and gave them a sedative (paregoric, which was a form of opium used as a pain reliever) to make them sleep when necessary.

At first, Harriet brought her charges only as far as Philadelphia. However, after the passage of the Fugitive Slave Law with the Compromise of 1850, no free northern city was a safe destination. Under this new law, any African American could be accused and arrested as a suspected runaway. The suspected slave would then go before a special United States commissioner. This official was paid five dollars for letting the suspect go free, but he got ten dollars for sending him or her south. Obviously, many unscrupulous officials opted for the more rewarding choice. Soon, the only safe place for former slaves was Canada. In 1833 the British, who ruled Canada at the time, had declared that all colored people living there were free. Harriet Tubman began bringing her people all the way to Canada—more than twice the length of the trip to Philadelphia. With the odds for recapture so much greater, she began to rely more and more on the Underground Railroad.

This network of helping hands, making up escape routes north, was called the Underground Railroad or Underground Road because the people involved did their work in secret. Various stories explain how it got its name. One involves a slave named Tice Davids who was fleeing from his master. Running through tangled underbrush, he came to the Ohio River and leaped in. His master clambered into a rowboat and took off after him, never letting his eyes off his slave. But when the master got to the far shore, Tice had disappeared. The slave owner searched high and low, but never found him. In exasperation, he exclaimed, "He must have gone on an underground road!"[6]

The Underground Railroad had been quietly operating for decades when Harriet Tubman escaped in 1849. The unmarked "road" ran through woods, over fields, and through swamps, with slaves being directed from one safe house, or station, to the next. The secret routes were most common in those northern states bordering the South: Delaware, Pennsylvania, Ohio, Illinois, and Indiana. Of the thousands of helpers on the Underground Railroad, many were African Americans. Most who gave a night's shelter or a ride to an escaping slave did so because of their belief that all people should be free. Every home, church, or schoolhouse where escaping slaves found shelter, food, clothing, or other help was considered part of the Underground Railroad. An estimated forty thousand to one hundred thousand slaves reached freedom via this invisible, interlocking road.[7] Many started their perilous trip by themselves, since it was dangerous to help fugitive slaves in the heart of slave country. Once they neared and then crossed the Mason-Dixon line, the Underground Railroad's closely woven network of support took over.

Only several dozen brave men and women of the Underground Railroad were willing to risk the journey south and actually lead a group of slaves all the way out. Harriet Tubman was one of them. Called

This painting by Charles T. Webber, entitled The Underground Railroad *shows escaped slaves being offered assistance on their journey toward freedom. Through this network of sympathetic northerners and safe houses, escaped slaves avoided being recaptured by their former owners.*

"conductors," they performed the most dangerous work on the Underground Railroad. Harriet Tubman used a dozen or so Underground Railroad stations in Delaware. Though it was dangerous to help fugitives in some areas, she always found people willing to help. The dangers and the help often cropped up unexpectedly. Early one morning, she arrived at one of the stations, the house of a free black man, who had often offered her and her charges shelter. She left her group huddled in the pouring rain and knocked her special rap, which was her signal, on his door. When nobody responded, she knocked again. Finally, a window was opened upstairs and a white man poked his head out. He demanded to know what she wanted. She asked for her friend and amid insults was informed that he had been forced out for hiding slaves. Realizing she was in danger of being caught, Tubman sought out a hiding place for herself and her group. She found one in a nearby swamp where they huddled, cold and damp, throughout the day. She spent the day praying for help. That evening, a man in Quaker dress sauntered along the path near the swamp and appeared to be talking quietly to himself. But he spoke just loudly enough for Tubman and her group to hear. He said that his wagon was in the nearby barnyard and there was a horse in the stable and a harness on a nail. When it was totally dark, Tubman found her way to the farm and found the wagon, filled with food, and she and her fugitives made their way safely to the next station.

Such narrow escapes deepened Harriet Tubman's faith. They also showed the effectiveness of the Underground Railroad. No escaping slave was ever captured while being led out by Harriet Tubman.[8] Most of the other conductors on the Underground

Railroad were stopped at least briefly. Some were arrested and jailed; others killed. Tubman was never caught, though she had some close calls. Maryland slave owners were determined to bring her in and tracked her constantly, offering a cash reward for whoever could catch her. Once, she was traveling north alone by train, having sent her escapees along ahead of her on the Underground Railroad. A passenger standing beside her began reading aloud a poster, or bulletin. It offered a reward for a runaway named Harriet Tubman. She kept her head down, departed the train at the next station, and hopped on board another one heading south. She thought nobody would look for a fugitive heading south.

Throughout her many dangerous exploits, she felt herself protected by God. She claimed she always went where he sent her. Once she and some fugitives were traveling up a road just south of Smyrna, Delaware. She said God told her to leave the road and turn left. She did and came to a stream. It was cold, but she was told to cross it. She did, and her group, reluctantly, followed her. She soon came to a cabin of freed men who offered to dry their clothes and provide them with food and shelter. Later, she discovered that farther down the road she had turned off was a slave patrol on the lookout for her and her group.

Call it divine protection, faith, or perhaps a sixth sense. Whatever it was, it kept Harriet Tubman safe. From 1852 to 1857, the woman whom her people came to call Moses returned over and over again to Maryland to bring out slaves. By late 1857, Harriet had freed her parents and all but one of her brothers and sisters. She generally made two trips a year, one in the spring and one in the fall, working the rest of the time to earn money for her trips. She sent the freed captives via the usual route to Philadelphia, then on to New York, to Syracuse and Rochester, and finally, to St. Catherine's in Ontario, Canada. Her work had been so successful that in some areas of Maryland the entire slave population had made its way to freedom.

6

A Nation Torn Apart—Slaves Are Freed

The Virginia countryside was muggy and sweltering on July 21, 1861. Here, by a slow-moving stream called Bull Run, armed troops were gathering for the first major battle of the Civil War. After years of tension, armed conflict had erupted between the North and South three months before. Eleven southern states, including Virginia, had withdrawn from the Union, formed their own Confederate government, and called up troops to defend themselves. Now, on this hot July day, the critical target was the town of Manassas Junction near Bull Run. It served as a key military outpost and as the main railroad junction for trains heading through the Blue Ridge Mountains to the Shenandoah Valley.

Determined to keep Manassas Junction under Confederate (southern) control, the flamboyant General P. T. Beauregard positioned his troops along the steep, wooded banks of Bull Run. Here, he and his men awaited the arrival of the enemy. They did not have to wait long. Setting out from Washington, D.C.,

were thousands of Union (northern) soldiers, the
biggest army ever called up in this country. They
headed along dirt roads through the low, rolling countryside of woods, fields, and farms toward Bull Run.
Several attacks and counterattacks proceeded. Before
long, a melee broke out. Five hundred Confederate
soldiers poured down the slope toward the Union
troops, letting loose with what would be called the
rebel yell—a high-pitched, raucous scream. This
screaming attack so disoriented the Union forces that
they were thrown into confusion. Still, the
Confederates took their share of a beating. Theirs was
a force of only fifty-five hundred men against an army
three times larger. "The balls just poured on us, struck
our muskets and hats and bodies," a Confederate soldier later confessed.[1] Another unit suffered equally, he
went on. "Our men fell constantly. The deadly missiles
rained like hail among the boughs and trees."[2] After
what appeared to be a Union victory, Confederate rein-
forcements arrived. Meantime, the Union forces had
scattered. They failed to come together in a single
decisive assault, which would have brought victory.
Instead, as the two armies surged back and forth in
charges and countercharges, the Union line fell apart.
By 4:30 P.M., the exhausted Union troops retreated in
panic. They had lost nearly five hundred men in the
course of the battle. Another thousand of them were
wounded and nearly two thousand either captured or
missing and presumed dead. Almost four hundred
Confederate soldiers lay dead with sixteen hundred
wounded.[3] Victory had gone to the South in this skir-
mish, known as the First Battle of Bull Run.

More important, this engagement showed all who
witnessed it the full horror of modern warfare. Few
were prepared for the actual toll of battle. The wounded

and dead lay strewn among the woods and fields. Many of the dead were missing heads or body parts. Others were groaning with pain. The Confederates, despite their victory, were too horrified by the slaughter to pursue the retreating Union troops. The reality of war hit home. Both sides would experience terrible suffering over the next four years.

Regional Differences Cause Friction

How had the nation come to this point? Why were Americans fighting one another in 1861? As we have seen, grave differences separated the North and South from the beginning. In the industrialized North, with its free labor force, the expansion of business, shipping, and industry made many rich and successful. In the more rural South, wealth was concentrated in the hands of a few. It was based on the production of crops grown on plantations and worked by slaves. Aside from these few slave owners, most of the white population in the South was poor. Many could neither read nor write.

The interests of this ruling white minority in the South were often opposed to those of the northern industrialists. The North supported public schools. Free public education would help improve all workers and add to business profits. The southern politicians wanted to keep the working classes ignorant. They feared that if the poor, whether black or white, became educated, they would perhaps challenge the white slave owners' control.[4]

The two sections had other points of disagreement. Northerners favored the use of national or federal government money for improvements in roads, canals, and railroads. The South wanted to control its own destiny without aid or interference from a strong federal government. It favored leaving most of the power in the hands of the states—a doctrine called states' rights. Some even said the South should separate itself from the rest of the country, or secede.

The Abolitionists Speak Out Against Slavery

As time went on, politics became mixed up with the slavery issue, driving a wedge between the two regions. Many people in the North held strong anti-slavery feelings. They formed organizations—more than one hundred altogether—dedicated to their cause. The abolitionists were the most extreme of these groups. They demanded slavery be abolished or ended immediately. Among the most outspoken of the abolitionists was a man named William Lloyd Garrison of Boston. In 1831 he founded the abolitionist newspaper, *The Liberator*. He proclaimed slavery a sin and all slave owners sinners. Garrison called for the immediate freeing, or emancipation, of all slaves. Many northern religious and political leaders, as well as free African Americans and whites, joined the abolitionist cause. They formed vigilance committees to protect runaway slaves. In Boston, crowds of abolitionists paraded through the streets. Clergy preached the cause of resisting slave-catching police by civil disobedience. Harriet Tubman received a great deal of support and help from these abolitionists and frequently spoke at their meetings, quietly telling her story. Others took great risks to aid fugitive slaves, many as participants in the Underground Railroad. One of these was a man named David Ruggles. He was a free African American in New York, dedicated to the cause. He repeatedly rescued slaves and helped them find jobs. He owned a bookstore and reading room. One day, proslavery people burned it down, probably because he had taught former slaves to read here. One of the fugitives he took in was a man named Frederick Augustus Washington Bailey. Bailey later changed his name to Frederick Douglass and dedicated himself to the abolitionist cause.

In 1852, at the height of the northern effort to help runaways, a fictional book called *Uncle Tom's Cabin* appeared. Written by a soft-spoken white woman named Harriet Beecher Stowe, it depicted the evils of slavery through the eyes of its main characters. Born in Connecticut, Harriet Beecher Stowe lived for a while in Ohio. There she saw slaves in chains being sent to auctions along the Ohio River. She never forgot the agonized look on a slave mother's face when her baby was wrenched from her. Harriet's sister-in-law urged her to write about the horrors of slavery. So that is what Harriet Beecher Stowe did. *Uncle Tom's Cabin* was the first popular piece of American literature that had an African American as the main character. Three hundred thousand copies of Stowe's book were sold in the first year.[5] Within four years, its sales topped those of any other book ever published in the United States except the Bible. *Uncle Tom's Cabin* became the abolitionists' single most influential work. It changed how many people thought about slavery. In much of the South, however, it was against the law to buy or own this book.

Southerners did not respond well to the abolitionists. Understandably, they resented being called sinners.[6] Further, calls for the immediate freeing of the slaves worried many. After all, by 1860, the total value of southern slaves was somewhere around 2 billion dollars.[7] Those who called for an end to slavery had no clear solutions about how to do this without causing the collapse of the entire southern economy.

Harriet Beecher Stowe was the author of the 1852 best-selling book Uncle Tom's Cabin. *The book helped unify northern sentiment against slavery, adding to the sectional conflict that ultimately inflamed the Civil War.*

Increasingly under attack, southerners closed ranks in defense of slavery. They viewed Harriet Beecher Stowe's novel as yet another insult to their way of life.[8] They feared the abolitionists' words and deeds might lead to a massive slave revolt. Partly in response to northern insults and partly out of economic need, the South determined to stand by its institution of slavery no matter what. While slavery was not the only serious difference between the North and South, it was the one that angered people so much that they could not discuss it calmly. Slavery was not the only cause of the Civil War, but it was the one without which the war most likely would never have occurred.[9]

The North and the South Move Farther Apart

By the mid-1850s, the spirit of accommodation between the North and the South, as symbolized by the Compromise of 1850, had practically vanished. The split between the two regions widened over more political fights related to the spread of slavery west into new territory. For example, in the late 1850s, violence broke out in Kansas, where a majority voted for this territory to become a free state. Proslavery forces refused to accept this decision, and fighting between the two sides erupted there. In 1856 fighting even occurred in the Senate. An antislavery senator, Charles Sumner of Massachusetts, was beaten unconscious with a cane by a proslavery representative from South Carolina named Preston Brooks.

Lincoln Is Elected President and the South Secedes

The final rift between the North and South was caused by the election of Abraham Lincoln as president in 1860. Lincoln was a Republican. The Republicans were a new party, opposed to slavery and to its extension westward. Elected on November 6, 1860, Lincoln was seen as a grave threat by southerners. They feared that the new president would limit or put an end to slavery. After years of threatening to pull out of the United States, many southern state officials began to seriously talk about secession. On December 20, 1860, South Carolina voted to secede. Within the next few months, Mississippi, Florida, Alabama, Georgia, Louisiana, and Texas also left. On February 8, 1861, the seven states that had withdrawn from the Union met at Montgomery, Alabama, to form a new nation, called the Confederate States of America. Their new constitution protected the right to own slaves in all their states and in any future territories. Jefferson Davis, a former soldier, congressman, senator, and secretary of war from Mississippi, was elected president of the new Confederacy.

The First Shots of the Civil War

At his inauguration on March 4, 1861 (in those days presidents were inaugurated four months after elected), Lincoln reminded the South of his oath of office. It obliged him to preserve, protect, and defend the Union. This included whatever forts or other possessions the United States government owned in the South. One such was Fort Sumter, a military post located in the harbor at Charleston, South Carolina. When Lincoln indicated he was sending supplies to the fort, the Confederates saw it as a challenge to their authority. On April 12, 1861, they opened fire on Fort Sumter, launching the first shots of the Civil War.

Neither Side Is Prepared

At or soon after the war's beginning, eleven southern states, including Virginia, North Carolina, and Tennessee, had joined the Confederacy. The total population of the secessionist states was 9 million, including 3.5 to 4 million slaves. The Union side consisted of twenty-three northern states with a total population of 22 million. The North had industry—factories to turn out essential goods such as weapons, rail ties, shoes, woolen clothing—and twice as many miles of railroads as the South.

Still, neither side was prepared for war. Neither realized ahead of time that the other was serious about fighting. When they did, it was too late to do anything but keep at it. The South had thought the North would just let it secede, since northerners appeared to hate slavery and slave owners. The North just figured the South was bluffing.[10] However, it soon became apparent that the Confederacy would fight for its independence. It was equally clear that the North would struggle to preserve the United States and the unity of the entire country.

Still, most people in both regions thought the war would last just a few months. They held a glamorous view of the whole thing. A civilian traveling on a train through the South in May 1861 wrote about his experience on the trains. They "were crowded with troops, and all as jubilant, as if they were going to a frolic, instead of a fight."[11] Bands played and crowds cheered as regiments marched off to the front. Many more rushed to enlist. Only after the Battle of Bull Run fiasco did the rosy image of a short, glorious, and bloodless war end and reality set in.

In the end, the North finally defeated the South. The human toll of these four years is staggering.

About 620,000 soldiers died—364,000 Union soldiers and 258,000 Confederates.[12] Private J. W. Reid from South Carolina wrote:

> I cannot give you an idea of the terrors of this battle. Try to picture . . . one hundred thousand men, all loading and firing as fast as they could. . . . The sight of the dead, the cries of the wounded, the thundering noise of the battle, can never be put on paper . . . some crying for water; some praying their last prayers; some trying to whisper to a friend their last farewell message to their loved ones at home. . . . Although the fight is over the field is yet quite red with blood.[13]

The Confederacy surrendered on April 9, 1865.

Emancipation

Several questions were resolved as a result of the northern victory. After this, no one state or states would have the power or right to break away from the United States. And the issue of slavery was determined. At the beginning of the war, President Lincoln believed that preserving the Union was more important than ending slavery. However, soon after the war had begun, many Republicans believed that abolishing slavery was an equally important cause. Some lawmakers said it would be a mockery if the Confederate rebellion were put down, but slavery still allowed. During the war, the whole slavery issue became more confused. Often they slaves fled from their owners, seeking freedom in the Union army camps. They were not always welcomed. Often they were met with cruelty or contempt in Union encampments.[14] Like many northerners, Union soldiers often opposed slavery in theory, but were unsympathetic to the slaves themselves.[15]

In early 1862, as the Civil War raged on, President Lincoln was under pressure from lawmakers in Congress to push toward the emancipation, or freeing of the slaves. Radical Republican Thaddeus Stevens led this effort. He said, "We must treat this [war] as a radical revolution."[16] He urged that Congress "free every slave. . . ." Lincoln moved cautiously. He was not in favor of slavery. As president, however, his job was to uphold the Constitution. The Constitution, as written at that time, protected slavery. Lincoln desperately needed the loyalty of the proslavery forces in the states bordering on the South, such as Maryland and Kentucky. When he appealed to congressmen from these states to approve a plan for the gradual freeing, or emancipation of the slaves, they refused to do so. These congressmen objected to the legality of Lincoln's plan. They feared that it would make the federal government too powerful. They also objected to the economic costs to slave owners. Lastly, they were anxious about what might happen if a large number of slaves suddenly gained their freedom.[17]

Nevertheless, Lincoln signed into law several bills to encourage gradual emancipation. For instance, one law said that slaves who came over to the Union side or ran away during the war were free. Further, it was unlawful to return fugitives from army camps to their masters. Thousands of slaves came under Union control, as a result. The Confiscation Act, passed in July 1862, made it legal to seize the property of southern rebels, including their slaves, who could be set free. This act was important as a symbol of how the purpose of the war in the North was shifting. It was no longer just aimed at bringing the South back into the Union. It was going to strike at the basis of the southern way of life. Gradually, Lincoln came around to this war goal. "The moment came," he said, "when I felt that slavery must die that the nation might live."[18] But he was cautious as to the timing of this drastic step.

Dead soldiers lie in front of Dunker Church on the Antietam battlefield in 1862. Matthew Brady, who accompanied Union armies during the Civil War, photographed the battle, which was the bloodiest of the war. Five days after this costly Union victory, Abraham Lincoln issued the Emancipation Proclamation.

The president decided to wait to announce the freeing of the slaves until the Union won a significant battle in the war. This would give the announcement more meaning. Lincoln's chance came in September 1862. Though more than half of the dead and wounded at the Battle of Antietam were Union soldiers, this bloody clash was a Northern victory. Within five days after Antietam, he issued a preliminary Emancipation Proclamation. In it, he warned the Confederate states that unless they came back into the Union by January 1, 1863, all slaves within the Confederacy would be declared free. Since none of the rebel states budged, Lincoln went ahead with the Emancipation Proclamation on January 1, 1863. "Fellow citizens, we cannot escape history. . . . The fiery trial through which we pass, will light us down, in honor or dishonor, to the latest generation. . . . In giving freedom to the slave, we assure freedom to the free."[19]

The Emancipation Proclamation was a revolutionary step. It won widespread approval in Europe, making the possibility of any European aid to the Confederate cause unlikely. It provided renewed hope for those enslaved, and it gave the Union a defined cause to fight for.

The Thirteenth Amendment

Ironically, the Emancipation Proclamation didn't actually free a single slave. The slaves it applied to were all in the rebel states, over which the Union laws had no effect. Many, including the president, questioned whether this proclamation, which was a wartime measure, could be legally enforced once the war ended. To ensure that it would be, it would have to become law in the form of an amendment to the Constitution. Lincoln and the Republicans in

Congress began to push for just such an amendment to abolish slavery. This Thirteenth Amendment was first proposed in April 1864. But the Democrats blocked it in the House of Representatives. It fell thirteen votes short of passing in June 1864. Politics over this issue became fierce and bitter.

Opponents objected to the revolutionary nature of federally decreed abolition. According to them it reduced the power of the states. Lincoln's reply was that he could no longer pursue "a temporizing and forbearing" policy toward the South.[20] To save the Union, he became convinced, he must destroy slavery. Indeed, by this time, the pressures for emancipation were tremendous.

Maryland and Missouri, two border states that had once resisted gradual emancipation, had come under control of a group of emancipationists. Before the war had ended, these states had passed laws abolishing slavery within their boundaries.[21] In 1864 Lincoln took the lead in making the Thirteenth Amendment part of the Republican party platform that would renominate him for president.[22] Finally in January 1865, about three months before the end of the war, the Thirteenth Amendment was passed in Congress. It was then sent to the states for approval and became part of the Constitution in December 1865. This amendment abolished slavery and gave Congress the power to pass laws to enforce the abolition.

Amendment Thirteen reads as follows:

Section 1. Neither slavery nor involuntary servitude, except as a punishment for crime whereof the party shall have been duly convicted, shall exist within the United States, or any place subject to their jurisdiction.

Section 2. Congress shall have power to enforce this article by appropriate legislation.

But laws could not abolish the attitudes that had reinforced slavery in the South for over three hundred years. It would take much more than a congressional amendment to undo that.

Reconstruction and Its Aftermath

The end of the Civil War and the Thirteenth Amendment gave nearly 4 million slaves their freedom.[1] Upon learning that they were free, many slaves sang and danced, whooped and hollered. One of them, named Charlotte Brown, of Wood's Crossing, Virginia, remembered all the rejoicing. But she noted, a few days later, on a Sunday, "We was all sitting roun' restin' and tryin' to think what freedom meant."[2]

That was an important question. Not just for the freed slaves, but also for the South and the United States as a whole. What did the Thirteenth Amendment and freedom mean for the millions of former slaves? What was next for them? Most did not know how to read or write. They had no money or jobs. Many thought that freedom meant they did not have to work anymore. Many lacked the skills to get a job. Others had no place to live. The war had destroyed many plantations, including the slave quarters. Thousands of slaves had left their masters during the Civil War to join the Union army as it marched through the South. Many of them were left with nowhere to go at war's end. Some still hung about the army. They camped in shacks or makeshift tents. Often they were sick or starving. Others, lacking a stable place to call home, had taken to the road in search of husbands, wives, or children whom they had lost due to slave trading or to the confusion of the war. One, a Reverend E. W. Johnson, placed an ad in a newspaper: "I have a mother somewhere in the world. I know not where. She used to belong to Philip Mathias in Elbert County, Georgia, and she left four of her children there about twenty-three years ago. . . . I heard she was carried off to Mississippi. . . ."[3]

In addition to the lack of money, shelter, work, and

Celebration among African Americans at the abolition of slavery in Washington, D.C., is shown in an 1866 engraving from Harper's. With emancipation came many

intact families, former slaves, or freedmen and freedwomen, as they were called, faced another obstacle to their rehabilitation. In a display of pure racism, almost all whites in the South (and nearly as many in the North) were opposed to granting freedmen and freedwomen equal rights.[4] White Americans had been raised to view blacks as inferior. Furthermore, many in the South had lost husbands, brothers, and sons in the Civil War. Since slavery had been a major cause of the war, white southerners blamed the former slaves for their personal losses. Having to adjust to a ravaged, defeated South, they clung to their old beliefs, refusing to change.

The period from 1865 until 1875 when people tried to rebuild the South is called Reconstruction, or the Reconstruction Era. A "reconstructed" South was supposed to include people of all races living together as equals. But despite laws toward this end and an attempt at this vision, it was never fully realized. The Reconstruction Era failed to grant equality and justice to the African American. It created more problems than it solved. The Thirteenth Amendment may have ended slavery, but the issue of racial equality could not be resolved through a constitutional amendment.

To assist former slaves in their struggle to become self-sufficient, Congress created the Freedmen's Bureau. It was a government agency set up to offer emergency help to those in need. The Freedmen's Bureau provided food and clothing to many, including some poor white people. It also funded schools for the former slaves. Before emancipation, it had been illegal in most southern states to teach slaves to read and write. Now, many African Americans eagerly wanted to learn. In Mississippi, former slaves jumped for joy when they heard that they were to have schools. Both children and parents flocked to these classrooms, set up wherever there was space—in barns, sheds, churches, and even outdoors in fields. At first, white missionaries and teachers sent south by northern churches or by the Freedmen's Bureau were in charge, along with a smattering of educated northern blacks. Before long, however, southern blacks began teaching each other. One former slave expressed a commonly held view, "My Lord, ma'am, what a great thing learning is!"[5] By 1870 there were four thousand new African-American schools in the South.[6] In addition, a dozen African-American colleges had opened up, including Fisk University in Nashville, Howard University in Washington, D.C., Hampton Institute in Hampton, Virginia, and Morehouse College in Atlanta. These excellent schools helped prepare young African Americans for a new life. Meantime, thousands of white southerners were so upset with the new social order that they fled the country for Mexico and South America.

President Lincoln, the man who had issued the Emancipation Proclamation and led the war to preserve the Union and uproot slavery from the South, was, sadly, no longer around to tackle the problems of a reconstructed South. He had had just a few days to enjoy the peace at war's end. On April 15, 1865, he died from an assassin's bullet. Upon Lincoln's death, Andrew Johnson, his vice-president, took over the highest office in the land. Johnson seemed indifferent to the fate of former slaves. Despite the existence of the Thirteenth Amendment, he ordered that all plantation lands be given back to their former owners, even though a law issued by the union General

Planters soon began seeking laborers for their lands. Many former slaves found the only kind of work they knew, as field hands. The new system, called sharecropping, was to prove almost as brutal as slavery. In theory, it seemed fair. A poor person, with farm skills, but no land, agreed to work the land of someone who had no cash to pay him or her. At harvest time, the landowner and the laborer were to divide the profits. But it rarely worked out that way. Black farmers, as well as poor white ones, worked small plots of land for the landowner. The landowner supplied his workers with seeds, tools, clothing, and food. The sharecropper purchased these on credit. The landowner also supplied the worker with a mule and a house—more often, a shack. The laborer paid rent on this shack. At the end of the growing season, the landlord sold the crop and pocketed his half of the profits. He deducted from the laborer's share all the rents, fees, and back credit owed him. This usually left the laborer with next to nothing. Sometimes, he ended up owing the landowner. The laborer often got more and more behind in his payments as years went by, slipping more and more into poverty. If the poor laborer tried to object to his treatment or tried to leave or get help elsewhere, he could be arrested or beaten or killed. Many former slaves who had stayed on their old plantations found themselves trapped in this sharecropping system, with little chance of escape.

To ensure that former slaves did not assume a dominant position in society, southern state governments began to pass discriminatory laws, called Black Codes. These laws said that freedmen and freedwomen could not vote. They could not move around freely from place to place. They could not mix with white people. And they could not attend public schools. Between

1865 and 1866, nearly every southern state passed Black Codes. About this same time, white patrols, similar to those used during slavery days, reappeared in the South. They consisted of armed white men on the lookout for suspicious-looking blacks. If there was no good excuse for the ex-slave to be out and about, he or she might be stopped, chased, shot, or hung. Black males, arrested for loitering, could be sentenced to farm camps. Here, they had to work as cheap laborers for white farmers or businesses. White southerners were determined to reassert the dominant role they had had before the war, and they seemed to be successfully doing so.[7]

When Congress met in December 1865, many of the nation's lawmakers were appalled at what was going on. How could this be? What was the purpose of the Civil War and of the Thirteenth Amendment? If it was to free the slaves, then why were the old slave masters being allowed to reenslave their former charges? Northern congressmen determined to set things right. Among those leading this effort was Congressman Thaddeus Stevens from Pennsylvania.

As a boy growing up in Vermont, Stevens had learned to be tough. He had been born with a deformed foot, called a clubfoot. It made him limp badly, and other kids often picked on him. To make matters worse, his father was an alcoholic who had abandoned the family when Thaddeus was young. The boy refused to be beaten by his circumstances. A bright student, he had a strong face with piercing hazel eyes and a shock of curly dark hair. When he left Vermont, at age twenty-four, he moved to Gettysburg, Pennsylvania. There, he became the best lawyer for respect of his neighbors, Stevens was elected to Congress, not just once, but over and over again. Starting in the 1830s, before the Civil War, he became an abolitionist. He would not sign the Pennsylvania constitution because it only allowed white people to vote. As lawyer to many fugitive slaves, Stevens refused to accept money for his aid. Nor was he afraid to say what was on his mind. Thaddeus Stevens felt that the southern states should not be admitted back into the Union until they gave former slaves the vote. Unfortunately, this would not happen for many years. Stevens also said that former slaves should be given land and guarantees of equality under the law. Without land, the freedmen and women would have little power and few opportunities to better themselves. Because many considered these demands radical, Stevens and his followers were called "Radical Republicans."

In Congress, Stevens became the main author of the Fourteenth Amendment. It was passed in June 1866. It gave citizenship to black Americans born in the United States. It said that no state could make a law that deprived any citizen of his or her basic rights or of equal protection under the law. Stevens pushed through Congress another law called the Reconstruction Act in March 1867. It said that the southern states could not participate in Congress until they had ratified the Fourteenth Amendment. It abolished the state governments filled with the ruling planter class. It divided the South into five military districts that were policed by the United States Army.

Unfortunately, Thaddeus Stevens never lived to see the passage of the Fifteenth Amendment, which said that the rights of United States citizens to vote shall not be denied or abridged on account of race, color, or previous enslavement. He had died two years before. After his death, his casket was placed in the Capitol building in Washington, D.C. Thousands paraded by to pay their respects. Stevens, at his own request, was buried in a cemetery where whites and blacks lay side by side. The message on his tombstone said that he had chosen to be buried here so that in death he might illustrate the same principles that had guided him in life.

Following the passage of the Fifteenth Amendment in 1870, African-American men by the thousands participated in elections for the first time ever. In some regions former slaves outnumbered white voters by a large margin. As a result, many African Americans were voted into office on the local, state, and national levels. Hiram Revels, a minister from Mississippi, was the first African American sent to the United States Senate. Between 1869 and 1873, seventeen African Americans were sent to Congress.[8] Well-educated and astute, they won widespread respect.

In reaction to the increased power of African Americans, white southerners retaliated. When Henry M. Turner was elected as a Georgia state lawmaker in 1868, his residency and other qualifications for office were questioned. Turner was an African-American minister, trained in the North. He had been a Union army chaplain during the Civil War. After the war's end, he lived in Georgia for nearly three years. Here, he worked for the African Methodist Episcopal Church, building churches and schools. The state of Georgia required that its lawmakers live for two years in the state before running for office. Turner had met

This Thomas Nast woodcut appeared in Harper's *in 1872. It depicts a black man who was killed by white southerners. In the years following the Civil War, anti-Reconstruction forces took to threats and violence in order to prevent African Americans from achieving any power in government and society.*

before the lawmakers. He refused, he said, to beg. He said he felt like a slave under the lash. He demanded his rights and angrily denounced those who would try to take them away. His self-defense withstood the efforts to topple him. He kept his seat and served out his term.[9]

Even nastier tactics were launched against other African-American officials. In 1868 James H. Alston, an African-American lawmaker in Alabama, was shot in his own bed. He counted 265 bullet holes on the outside of his house, five through the headboard of his bed, and two that actually hit him.[10] Intimidation failed, for a time, to stop African Americans from voting and from electing their own representatives.

Toward the end of the Reconstruction Era, one last law was enacted by Congress to help the former slaves. This was the Civil Rights Act of 1875. It prohibited segregation—the practice of keeping African Americans apart from whites because of their skin color. This law said all persons were entitled to equal enjoyment of hotels, public transportation, and public parks and theaters. All persons, regardless of race, were allowed to be jurors in all courts. The Reconstructionists in Congress had passed a number of laws to try to make the former slaves equal and protected under the law. Their efforts were soon to come unraveled, however.

Most white southerners ignored the Civil Rights Act. In 1883 the United States Supreme Court declared most of it illegal. (Amazingly, it was not until 1957, some sixty years later, that new laws were passed protecting African Americans' rights.) By the time federal troops were withdrawn from the South in 1877, support for sustaining these gains and enforcing the law in the South waned. Into this vacuum charged the white southerners. They gradually won back the power they had lost during the period 1865 to 1875. Slowly, the governments instituted under Reconstruction began to crumble. By the 1890s white southerners had figured out new ways to keep African Americans from voting. Whites set up conditions that had to be met before a black man (women did not yet have the vote) could register to vote. The black voter was slowly deprived of the vote. In Louisiana the number of registered African-American voters declined from 130,334 in 1896 to 1,342 in 1904.[11]

Other laws called "Jim Crow" laws reasserted the dominant position of the white majority in the South in the 1890s. Jim Crow was an insult when applied to African Americans. The laws cast African Americans into separateness. They required them to live apart and to avoid mingling with whites. They were to stay away from the hotels, restaurants, and schools that whites used. The new segregation had its most devastating effect in the field of education. Separate hardly ever meant equal. As late as 1945, many southern school districts did not provide for the required twelve years of public education for African Americans.[12] School facilities were inferior to those for whites; the same was true of the restrooms, waiting rooms, and other facilities allotted to African Americans.

By 1900 African Americans were rendered separate and unequal to varying degrees in both the South and the North. Many were not much better off than they had been once as slaves. True, nowhere in the world at this time was there a fair-minded, interracial society: not in Europe, Asia, or Africa.[13] The first step had been taken with the passage of the Thirteenth,

Fourteenth, and Fifteenth Amendments. Yet in the end, African Americans in the South—and to a lesser extent in the North—continued to be abused and put down. It would be another half century or more before the beginnings of justice would be served the descendants of the former slaves.

Looking Toward the Future

Sometimes ordinary people can change the course of history. Rosa Parks was one such person. A seamstress at a department store in Montgomery, Alabama, Parks was a short, soft-spoken woman who wore wire-rimmed glasses and pulled her hair up into a bun. She rode the bus to and from work every day. In Montgomery, as elsewhere in the South in the early 1900s, the buses were segregated. Blacks had to sit in the back while whites sat in the front. If a white person needed a seat, and there was none up front, the driver would often order a black person to give up his or her seat. Often as many as three or four blacks had to stand to accommodate one white person, because blacks and whites could not sit in the same row together.

On December 1, 1955, Rosa Parks was on a bus, heading home from work. She had become an active member of the state National Association for the Advancement of Colored People (NAACP). This organization was founded in 1909 to advance the rights of African Americans. In 1954 Parks had taken a workshop on ways to fight discrimination. This particular evening, she was tired. She was glad she had a seat on the bus. She had not planned on making a dramatic gesture. Like most other African Americans in Montgomery, she had experienced many small injustices while riding the bus. In fact, this time when she boarded the bus, she recognized the bus driver. He had humiliated her not long before. African-American riders had to pay their money at the front of the bus, then disembark, and board at the back door. They were not allowed to walk down the aisle of the bus to take their seats in the back. A while ago, Rosa Parks had boarded a bus at the front, paid her money, then gotten off. But as she walked back to board it again, the bus driver had simply driven off, leaving her standing there on the sidewalk.

This particular evening, she realized it was the same driver. After Parks boarded, the seats on the bus filled up quickly. A white man climbed on, and the bus driver told the black passengers in Parks's row to stand. Everyone grudgingly obeyed—everyone, that is, except Rosa Parks. She had had enough of being bossed around. The bus driver started shouting at her to stand up. When she refused to budge, he threatened to have her arrested. Still, she stayed put. Soon, the police came and arrested Parks. She was taken off the bus and sent to jail.

One of Rosa Parks's friends, E. D. Dixon, was the head of the Alabama branch of the NAACP. He put up the money to get Parks out of jail. She would still have to go to court for breaking the law. Dixon asked her if

Rosa Parks gazes out the window of a bus. Parks was arrested on December 1, 1955, for sitting in a whites-only section of a Montgomery, Alabama, bus. Her arrest touched off a year-long boycott of the bus system by African Americans.

the Ku Klux Klan or other angry whites. Still, she was tired of the humiliation of segregation.

Change was slow to come. After World War II ended in 1945, some of the half million African-American soldiers who had fought for their country overseas began returning home. Many were incensed that they had put their lives on the line for a country in which discrimination and segregation persisted. Some pushed for change. Despite the passage of three constitutional amendments, the first real victories for African Americans were in the courts. In 1950 lawyers for the NAACP began to prepare a case that would mark the beginning of the modern civil rights movement. They were determined to prove that segregated schools were unfair and should be illegal. They took their case, *Brown* v. *Board of Education*, all the way to the Supreme Court, and they won. In May 1954, the Supreme Court ruled that segregated schools were "inherently unequal." Even if separate black schools had the same physical facilities as white ones—which was rare—the Court ruled there was no true equality, as long as they were separate. It would take more government action and more than a decade before southern schools would become fully integrated, but this ruling had weakened the Jim Crow laws. Change was bound to follow.

It was seven months after *Brown* v. *Board of Education* that Rosa Parks committed her small act of rebellion on a Montgomery bus. Her protest touched off an avalanche. African-American leaders took her arrest as a good reason to fight for change. They organized a citywide boycott of the buses on December 5, would have to walk or find rides. White violence was a real fear. But amazingly, almost all blacks stayed off the buses on December 5. And the next day. And the day after that. Pretty soon a month had gone by, and still the city's buses were half empty. African-American passengers stayed off the buses for months, in the rain and cold of winter and throughout the brutal humidity and heat of the following summer. White leaders tried force to combat the boycott. They arrested and jailed many. Angry whites took things in their own hands. They burned down and bombed black homes and churches. But none of this put an end to the bus boycott. Resolved to hang on until segregation and discrimination on their buses ended, African Americans stayed off Montgomery's buses.

Their leader in this struggle soon took the national spotlight. He was a twenty-six-year-old charismatic minister named Martin Luther King, Jr. "There comes a time that people get tired," King said.[2] "We are here . . . to say to those who have mistreated us so long that we are tired—tired of being segregated and humiliated; tired of being kicked about by the brutal feet of oppression. We have no alternative but to protest."[3] King's technique was called nonviolent protest. He urged the boycotters to use nothing but peaceful methods, and not respond to hate with hate. He and his wife, Coretta Scott King, were arrested for leading the boycott. Still, he kept preaching peace. White people screamed at blacks, threw rocks, kicked in tires, and burned and bombed things belonging to blacks. King and his boycotters did not yell back. They did not respond at all. They kept cool and calm. Soon, television camera crews, newspaper reporters, and commentators from around the country and the world were flocking to Montgomery to report on this story.

At last, thirteen months after Rosa Parks's arrest, the Supreme Court ruled that segregation on Alabama buses was illegal and unconstitutional. This victory had far-reaching importance. It showed that poor and middle-class African Americans could unite and, by nonviolent means, overturn injustices in the South. From then on, peaceful protest would become the major method of the growing civil rights movement. Martin Luther King, Jr., would be its guiding light and, to many, the most inspiring and powerful African-American leader of the century.

Using Montgomery as a model, blacks and their white supporters staged numerous protests throughout the country. School segregation became the next battleground. Despite the Supreme Court's 1954 ruling declaring segregated schools illegal, most cities refused to comply with the law and integrate their schools. School officials in Little Rock, Arkansas, tried to abide by the Supreme Court's ruling. In September 1957, they planned to admit nine African-American students to Central High School as a first step. Up until then, the school, considered one of the finest high schools in the country, had never had a black student. Orville Faubus, governor of Arkansas, refused to cooperate with Little Rock school officials. He did not want to integrate the schools in his state. He was afraid of losing white votes in the next election. He ordered the state National Guard to block the entrance of the nine black students to Central High.

One of the African American girls who planned to

school together. Her family did not have a telephone, so there was no way to tell her this. She arrived at school alone. Clutching her books and proudly wearing a new dress, she was met by a mob of white people. They started yelling and jeering. One woman spat at her. Some boys told her they were going to lynch her. With great dignity, she walked toward the school's entrance. But in the face of all this hate, she panicked and ran back to a bench by the curb, where she collapsed sobbing. A reporter came up to her and put his arm around her, and whispered for her not to cry. With the help of a sympathizer in the crowd, she left and went home.

Three weeks later, President Eisenhower sent United States Army troops to Little Rock to allow the "Little Rock Nine," as the African-American students were called, to attend Central High. A convoy of jeeps and soldiers guarded by helicopters escorted the students to school. One of the students, Ernest Green, recalled that day. "We marched up the steps . . . with this circle of soldiers with bayonets drawn. . . . Walking up the steps that day was probably one of the biggest feelings I've ever had."[5] Later that year, Ernest became the first African American to graduate from Central High. He knew he was forging a revolution when he received his diploma. And he was right.

Soon after Little Rock, thousands of young people began leading peaceful sit-ins against segregated parks, libraries, movie theaters, bus stations, and swimming pools in many southern cities. Calm and courageous in the face of taunts, many participants were kicked, clubbed, and burned by cigarette butts. Some were even murdered, but no amount of resistance could hold back the tide of the civil rights movement now.

More than two hundred thousand people protested continued discrimination in a huge march on Washington, held August 28, 1963. Large-scale demonstrations were held in Birmingham, Alabama, in April 1963, and in Selma, Alabama, in March 1965. Many law officials responded with brutal means, bringing out attack dogs and spraying marchers with high-powered fire hoses. Sometimes, officials simply refused to protect the demonstrators, who were often beaten. Violence escalated each time the protesters won a victory, with bombings and murders by angry white supremacists. In 1968, Martin Luther King, Jr., was assassinated in Memphis, Tennessee. After his death, widespread rioting and looting occurred in many American cities, reflecting the rage and despair of many at the loss of their beloved leader.

The federal government responded to the protests and violence by passing several laws aimed at ending segregation and protecting African Americans' rights. The most significant were the Civil Rights Act of 1964, prohibiting discrimination against African Americans, and the Voting Rights Act of 1965, ensuring the federal government's support of African American voting rights.

The end of the 1960s saw a rise in African-American awareness and in the more aggressive civil rights groups, such as the Black Panther party and the Black Muslims. Since then, African Americans have made huge strides in many fields. Thousands are active voters with a major voice in the outcome of

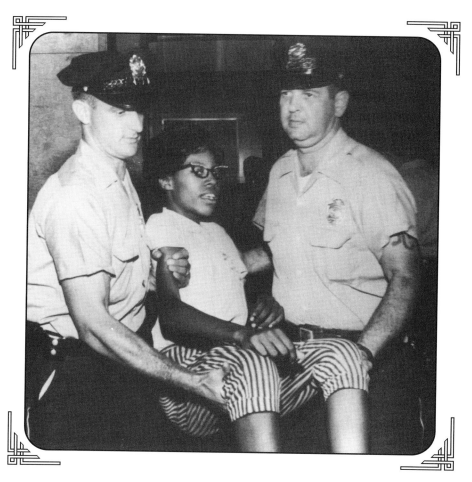

In East St. Louis, Illinois, police carry an African-American young woman from the doorway of a bank. She and other members of the youth committee of the NAACP had been protesting the bank's biased hiring practices. Protests and sit-ins like this one were common in the civil rights era.

last three decades, more than a dozen African Americans have served as mayors of American cities. Some forty of them have become congressmen and congresswomen and many have served in high-ranking federal government positions.[6]

Still, despite all these gains, African Americans have not achieved full equality in all areas of society, nor has racial hatred ceased. The average income level of African Americans in this country is significantly below that of whites. The ghettoes of our cities are riddled with run-down housing, drugs, and poverty. The daily newspapers are filled with stories of conflict between blacks and whites.

Perhaps, we should follow the example set by the residents of Sandpoint, Idaho. A small town of only some five thousand people, it has recently drawn a considerable number of newcomers, who are drawn to its open spaces and clean air. Some are members of organized militia groups who believe white people are superior to other races. Others teach that nonwhites and non-Christians do not deserve respect. When racist graffiti began to appear on buildings in Sandpoint, and hate mail started to arrive in the residents' mailboxes, Sandpoint decided to take action. A group of residents formed a Human Rights Task Force. They went door-to-door delivering a message of tolerance and informing townspeople about their educational programs aimed at fostering harmony between peoples. They met with some of the newcomers and convinced them to seek nonviolent solutions to their differences. Sandpoint children created holiday cards showing scenes of racial unity as part of an "Art for Tolerance" contest. The contest winner, a seventh grader named Ashley Howell, wisely noted, "If we grow up having negative attitudes about people, we'll have those dangerous attitudes all our lives."[7]

Despite the passage of the Thirteenth Amendment, the shackles of slavery still encumber our society, often in subtle, deeply rooted ways. We can all look within and examine our negative attitudes toward people who are different from us. We can unlearn our prejudices. It is up to each of us to create a place in our hearts and in the world that allows for—indeed welcomes—differences between people.

The Constitution of the United States

The text of the Constitution is presented here. All words are given their modern spelling and capitalization. Brackets [ ] indicate parts that have been changed or set aside by amendments.

Preamble

We the people of the United States, in order to form a more perfect Union, establish justice, insure domestic tranquility, provide for the common defense, promote the general welfare, and secure the blessings of liberty to ourselves and our posterity, do ordain and establish this Constitution for the United States of America.

ARTICLE I
The Legislative Branch

Section 1. All legislative powers herein granted shall be vested in a Congress of the United States, which shall consist of a Senate and House of Representatives.

The House of Representatives

Section 2. (1) The House of Representatives shall be composed of members chosen every second year by the people of the several states, and the electors in each state shall have the qualifications requisite for electors of the most numerous branch of the state legislature.

(2) No person shall be a representative who shall not have attained the age of twenty-five years, and been seven years a citizen of the United States, and who shall not, when elected, be an inhabitant of that state in which he shall be chosen.

(3) Representatives and direct taxes shall be apportioned among the several states which may be included within this Union, according to their respective numbers, [which shall be determined by adding to the whole number of free persons, including those bound to service for a term of years, and excluding Indians not taxed, three-fifths of all other persons]. The actual enumeration shall be made within three years after the first meeting of the Congress of the United States, and within every subsequent term of ten years, in such manner as they shall by law direct. The number of representatives shall not exceed one for every thirty thousand, but each state shall have at least one representative; [and until such enumeration shall be made, the state of New Hampshire shall be entitled to choose three, Massachusetts eight, Rhode Island and Providence Plantations one, Connecticut five, New York six, New Jersey four, Pennsylvania eight, Delaware one, Maryland six, Virginia ten, North Carolina five, South Carolina five, and Georgia three].

(4) When vacancies happen in the representation from any state, the executive authority thereof shall issue writs of election to fill such vacancies.

(5) The House of Representatives shall choose their Speaker and other officers; and shall have the sole power of impeachment.

The Senate

Section 3. (1) The Senate of the United States shall be composed of two senators from each state, [chosen by the legislature thereof,] for six years; and each senator shall have one vote.

(2) Immediately after they shall be assembled in consequence of the first election, they shall be divided as equally as may be into three classes. The seats of the senators of the first class shall be vacated at the expiration of the second year, of the second class at the expiration of the fourth year, and of the third class at the expiration of the sixth year, so that one-third may be chosen every second year; [and if vacancies happen by resignation, or otherwise, during the recess of the legislature of any state, the executive thereof may make temporary appointments until the next meeting of the legislature, which shall then fill such vacancies].

(3) No person shall be a senator who shall not have attained to the age of thirty years, and been nine years a citizen of the United States, and who shall not, when elected, be an inhabitant of that state for which he shall be chosen.

(4) The Vice President of the United States shall be president of the Senate, but shall have no vote, unless they be equally divided.

(5) The Senate shall choose their other officers, and also a president *pro tempore*, in the absence of the Vice President, or when he shall exercise the office of President of the United States.

(6) The Senate shall have the sole power to try all impeachments. When sitting for that purpose, they shall be on oath or affirmation. When the President of the United States is tried, the Chief Justice shall preside: and no person shall be convicted without the concurrence of two-thirds of the members present.

(7) Judgement in cases of impeachment shall not extend further than to removal from office, and disqualification to hold and enjoy any office of honor, trust, or profit under the United States: but the party convicted shall nevertheless be liable and subject to indictment, trial, judgement and punishment, according to law.

Organization of Congress

Section 4. (1) The times, places and manner of holding elections for senators and representatives, shall be prescribed in each state by the legislature thereof; but the Congress may at any time by law make or alter such regulations, [except as to the places of choosing senators].

(2) The Congress shall assemble at least once in every year, [and such meeting shall be on the first Monday in December], unless they shall by law appoint a different day.

Section 5. (1) Each house shall be the judge of the elections, returns and qualifications of its own members, and a majority of each shall constitute a quorum to do business; but a smaller number may adjourn from day to day, and may be authorized to compel the attendance of absent members, in such manner, and under such penalties as each house may provide.

(2) Each house may determine the rules of its proceedings, punish its members for disorderly behavior, and, with the concurrence of two-thirds, expel a member.

(3) Each house shall keep a journal of its proceedings, and from time to time publish the same, excepting such parts as may in their judgement require secrecy; and the yeas and nays of the members of either house on any question shall, at the desire of one-fifth of those present, be entered on the journal.

(4) Neither house, during the session of Congress, shall, without the consent of the other, adjourn for more than three days, nor to any other place than that in which the two houses shall be sitting.

Section 6. (1) The senators and representatives shall receive a compensation for their services, to be ascertained by law, and paid out of the treasury of the United States. They shall in all cases, except treason, felony and breach of the peace, be privileged from arrest during their attendance at the session of their respective houses, and in going to and returning from the same; and for any speech or debate in either house, they shall not be questioned in any other place.

(2) No senator or representative shall, during the time for which he was elected, be appointed to any civil office under the authority of the United States, which shall have been created, or the emoluments whereof shall have been increased during such time; and no person holding any office under the United States shall be a member of either house during his continuance in office.

Section 7. (1) All bills for raising revenue shall originate in the House of Representatives; but the Senate may propose or concur with amendments as on other bills.

(2) Every bill which shall have passed the House of Representatives and the Senate, shall, before it become a law, be presented to the President of the United States; if he approve he shall sign it, but if not he shall return it, with his objections to that house in which it shall have originated, who shall enter the objections at large on their journal, and proceed to reconsider it. If after such reconsideration two-thirds of that house shall agree to pass the bill, it shall be sent, together with the objections, to the other house, by which it shall likewise be reconsidered, and if approved by two-thirds of that house, it shall become a law. But in all such cases the votes of both houses shall be determined by yeas and nays, and the names of the persons voting for and against the bill shall be entered on the journal of each house respectively. If any bill shall not be returned by the President within ten days (Sundays excepted) after it shall have been presented to him, the same shall be a law, in like manner as if he had signed it, unless the Congress by their

adjournment prevent its return, in which case it shall not be a law.

(3) Every order, resolution, or vote to which the concurrence of the Senate and House of Representatives may be necessary (except on a question of adjournment) shall be presented to the President of the United States; and before the same shall take effect, shall be approved by him, or being disapproved by him, shall be repassed by two-thirds of the Senate and House of Representatives, according to the rules and limitations prescribed in the case of a bill.

Powers Granted to Congress

The Congress shall have power:

Section 8. (1) To lay and collect taxes, duties, imposts and excises, to pay the debts and provide for the common defense and general welfare of the United States; but all duties, imposts and excises shall be uniform throughout the United States;

(2) To borrow money on the credit of the United States;

(3) To regulate commerce with foreign nations, and among the several states, and with the Indian tribes;

(4) To establish an uniform rule of naturalization, and uniform laws on the subject of bankruptcies throughout the United States;

(5) To coin money, regulate the value thereof, and of foreign coin, and fix the standard of weights and measures;

(6) To provide for the punishment of counterfeiting the securities and current coin of the United States;

(7) To establish post offices and post roads;

(8) To promote the progress of science and useful arts, by securing for limited times to authors and inventors the exclusive right to their respective writings and discoveries;

(9) To constitute tribunals inferior to the Supreme Court;

(10) To define and punish piracies and felonies committed on the high seas, and offenses against the law of nations;

(11) To declare war, grant letters of marque and reprisal, and make rules concerning captures on land and water;

(12) To raise and support armies, but no appropriation of money to that use shall be for a longer term than two years;

(13) To provide and maintain a navy;

(14) To make rules for the government and regulation of the land and naval forces;

(15) To provide for calling forth the militia to execute the laws of the Union, suppress insurrections and repel invasions;

(16) To provide for organizing, arming, and disciplining the militia, and for governing such part of them as may be employed in the service of the United States, reserving to the states respectively, the appointment of the officers, and the authority of training the militia according to the discipline prescribed by Congress;

(17) To exercise exclusive legislation in all cases whatsoever, over such district (not exceeding ten miles square) as may, by cession of particular states, and the acceptance of Congress, become the seat of the government of the United States, and to exercise like authority over all places purchased by the consent of the legislature of the state in which the same shall be, for the erection of forts, magazines, arsenals, dockyards, and other needful buildings;—And

(18) To make all laws which shall be necessary and proper for carrying into execution the foregoing powers, and all other powers vested by this Constitution in the government of the United States, or in any department or officer thereof.

Powers Forbidden to Congress

Section 9. (1) The migration or importation of such persons as any of the states now existing shall think proper to admit, shall not be prohibited by the Congress prior to the year one thousand eight hundred and eight, but a tax or duty may be imposed on such importation, not exceeding ten dollars for each person.

(2) The privilege of the writ of *habeas corpus* shall not be suspended, unless when in cases of rebellion or invasion the public safety may require it.

(3) No bill of attainder or *ex post facto* law shall be passed.

(4) No capitation, [or other direct,] tax shall be laid, unless in proportion to the census or enumeration herein before directed to be taken.

(5) No tax or duty shall be laid on articles exported from any state.

(6) No preference shall be given by any regulation of commerce or revenue to the ports of one state over those of another: nor shall vessels bound to, or from, one state, be obliged to enter, clear, or pay duties in another.

(7) No money shall be drawn from the treasury, but in consequence of appropriations made by law; and a regular statement and account of the receipts and expenditures of all public money shall be published from time to time.

(8) No title of nobility shall be granted by the United States: And no person holding any office or profit or trust under them, shall, without the consent of the Congress, accept of any present, emolument, office, or title, of any kind whatsoever, from any king, prince, or foreign state.

Powers Forbidden to the States

Section 10. (1) No state shall enter into any treaty, alliance, or confederation; grant letters of marque and reprisal; coin money; emit bills of credit; make any thing but gold and silver coin a tender in payment of debts; pass any bill of attainder, *ex post facto* law, or law impairing the obligation of contracts, or grant any title of nobility.

(2) No state shall, without the consent of the Congress, lay any imposts or duties on imports or exports, except what may be absolutely necessary for executing its inspection laws: and the net produce of all duties and imposts, laid by any state on imports or exports, shall be for the use of the treasury of the United States, and all such laws shall be subject to the revision and control of the Congress.

(3) No state shall, without the consent of Congress, lay any duty of tonnage, keep troops, or ships of war in time of peace, enter into any agreement or compact with another state, or with a foreign power, or engage in war, unless actually invaded, or in such imminent danger as will not admit of delay.

Article II
The Executive Branch

Section 1. (1) The executive power shall be vested in a President of the United States of America. He shall hold his office during the term of four years, and, together with the Vice President, chosen for the same term, be elected as follows:

(2) Each state shall appoint, in such manner as the legislature thereof may direct, a number of electors, equal to the whole number of senators and representatives to which the state may be entitled in the Congress: but no senator or representative, or person holding an office of trust or profit under the United States, shall be appointed an elector.

(3) [The electors shall meet in their respective states, and vote by ballot for two persons, of whom one at least shall not be an inhabitant of the same state with themselves. And they shall make a list of all the persons voted for, and of the number of votes for each; which list they shall sign and certify, and transmit sealed to the seat of government of the United States, directed to the president of the Senate. The president of the Senate shall, in the presence of the Senate and House of Representatives, open all the certificates, and the votes shall then be counted. The person having the greatest number of votes shall be the President, if such number be a majority of the whole number of electors appointed; and if there be more than one who have such majority, and have an equal number of votes, then the House of Representatives shall immediately choose by ballot one of them for President; and if no person have a majority, then from the five highest on the list the said House shall in like manner choose the President. But in choosing the President, the votes shall be taken by states, the representation from each state having one vote; a quorum for this purpose shall consist of a member or members from two-thirds of the states, and a majority of all the states shall be necessary to a choice. In every case, after the choice of the President, the person having the greatest number of votes of the electors shall be the Vice President. But if there should remain two or more who have equal votes, the Senate shall choose from them by ballot the Vice President.]

(4) The Congress may determine the time of choosing the electors, and the day on which they shall give their

votes; which day shall be the same throughout the United States.

(5) No person except a natural-born citizen, or a citizen of the United States, at the time of the adoption of this Constitution, shall be eligible to the office of President; neither shall any person be eligible to that office who shall not have attained to the age of thirty-five years, and been fourteen years a resident within the United States.

(6) In case of the removal of the President from office, or of his death, resignation, or inability to discharge the powers and duties of the said office, the same shall devolve on the Vice President, and the Congress may by law provide for the case of removal, death, resignation, or inability, both of the President and Vice President, declaring what officer shall then act as President, and such officer shall act accordingly, until the disability be removed, or a President shall be elected.

(7) The President shall, at stated times, receive for his services, a compensation, which shall neither be increased nor diminished during the period for which he shall have been elected, and he shall not receive within that period any other emolument from the United States, or any of them.

(8) Before he enter on the execution of his office, he shall take the following oath or affirmation: "I do solemnly swear (or affirm) that I will faithfully execute the office of the President of the United States, and will to the best of my ability, preserve, protect and defend the Constitution of the United States."

Section 2. (1) The President shall be commander-in-chief of the Army and Navy of the United States, and of the militia of the several states, when called into the actual service of the United States; he may require the opinion, in writing, of the principal officer in each of the executive departments, upon any subject relating to the duties of their respective offices, and he shall have power to grant reprieves and pardons for offenses against the United States, except in cases of impeachment.

(2) He shall have power, by and with the advice and consent of the Senate, to make treaties, provided two-thirds of the senators present concur; and he shall nominate, and by and with the advice and consent of the Senate, shall appoint ambassadors, other public ministers and consuls, judges of the Supreme Court, and all other officers of the United States, whose appointments are not herein otherwise provided for, and which shall be established by law: but the Congress may by law vest the appointment of such inferior officers, as they think proper, in the President alone, in the courts of law, or in the heads of departments.

(3) The President shall have the power to fill up all vacancies that may happen during the recess of the Senate, by granting commissions which shall expire at the end of their next session.

Section 3. He shall from time to time give to the Congress information of the state of the Union, and recommend to their consideration such measures as he shall judge necessary and expedient; he may, on extraordinary occasions, convene both houses, or either of them, and in case of disagreement between them, with respect to the time of adjournment, he may adjourn them to such time as he shall think proper; he shall receive ambassadors and other public ministers; he shall take care that the laws be faithfully executed, and shall commission all the officers of the United States.

Section 4. The President, Vice President and all civil officers of the United States, shall be removed from office on impeachment for, and conviction of, treason, bribery, or other high crimes and misdemeanors.

ARTICLE III
The Judicial Branch

Section 1. The judicial power of the United States, shall be vested in one Supreme Court, and in such inferior courts as the Congress may from time to time ordain and establish. The judges, both of the Supreme and inferior courts, shall hold their offices during good behaviour, and shall, at stated times, receive for their services, a compensation, which shall not be diminished during their continuance in office.

Section 2. (1) The judicial power shall extend to all cases, in law and equity, arising under this Constitution, the laws of the United States, and treaties made, or which shall be made, under their authority; —to all cases affecting ambassadors, other public ministers and consuls;—to all cases of admiralty and maritime jurisdiction;—to controversies to which the United States shall be a party;—to controversies between two or more states, [between a state and citizens of another state;], between citizens of different states;—between citizens of the same state claiming lands under grants of different states, and between a state, or the citizens thereof, and foreign states, [citizens or subjects].

(2) In all cases affecting ambassadors, other public ministers and consuls, and those in which a state shall be party, the Supreme Court shall have original jurisdiction. In all the other cases before mentioned, the Supreme Court shall have appellate jurisdiction, both as to law and fact, with such exceptions, and under such regulations as the Congress shall make.

(3) The trial of all crimes, except in cases of impeachment, shall be by jury; and such trial shall be held in the state where the said crimes shall have been committed; but when not committed within any state, the trial shall be at such place or places as the Congress may by law have directed.

Section 3. (1) Treason against the United States, shall consist only in levying war against them, or in adhering to their enemies, giving them aid and comfort. No person shall be convicted of treason unless on the testimony of two witnesses to the same overt act, or on confession in open court.

(2) The Congress shall have power to declare the punishment of treason, but no attainder of treason shall work corruption of blood, or forfeiture, except during the life of the person attainted.

ARTICLE IV
Relation of the States to Each Other

Section 1. Full faith and credit shall be given in each state to the public acts, records, and judicial proceedings of every other state. And the Congress may by general laws prescribe the manner in which such acts, records and proceedings shall be proved, and the effect thereof.

Section 2. (1) The citizens of each state shall be entitled to all privileges and immunities of citizens in the several states.

(2) A person charged in any state with treason, felony, or other crime, who shall flee justice, and be found in another state, shall on demand of the executive authority of the state from which he fled, be delivered up, to be removed to the state having jurisdiction of the crime.

(3) [No person held to service or labor in one state, under the laws thereof, escaping into another, shall, in consequence of any law or regulation therein, be discharged from such service or labor, but shall be delivered up on claim of the party to whom such service or labor may be due.]

Federal-State Relations

Section 3. (1) New states may be admitted by the Congress into this Union; but no new state shall be formed or erected within the jurisdiction of any other state, nor any state be formed by the junction of two or more states, without the consent of the legislatures of the states concerned as well as of the Congress.

(2) The Congress shall have power to dispose of and make all needful rules and regulations respecting the territory or other property belonging to the United States; and nothing in this Constitution shall be so construed as to prejudice any claims of the United States, or of any particular state.

Section 4. The United States shall guarantee to every state in this Union a republican form of government, and shall protect each of them against invasion; and on application of the legislature, or of the executive (when the legislature cannot be convened), against domestic violence.

ARTICLE V
Amending the Constitution

The Congress, whenever two-thirds of both houses shall deem it necessary, shall propose amendments to this Constitution, or, on the application of the legislatures of two-thirds of the several states, shall call a convention for proposing amendments, which, in either case, shall be valid to all intents and purposes, as part of this Constitution, when ratified by the legislatures of three-fourths of the several states, or by conventions in three-fourths thereof, as the one or the other mode of ratification may be proposed by the Congress; provided [that no amendment which may be made prior to the year one thousand eight hundred and eight, shall in any manner affect the first and fourth clauses in the ninth section of the first article; and] that no state, without its consent, shall be deprived of its equal suffrage in the Senate.

ARTICLE VI
National Debts

(1) All debts contracted and engagements entered into, before the adoption of this Constitution, shall be as

valid against the United States under this Constitution, as under the Confederation.

Supremacy of the National Government

(2) This Constitution, and the laws of the United States which shall be made in pursuance thereof; and all treaties made, or which shall be made, under the authority of the United States shall be the supreme law of the land; and the judges in every state shall be bound thereby, any thing in the constitution or laws of any state to the contrary notwithstanding.

(3) The senators and representatives before mentioned, and the members of the several state legislatures, and all executive and judicial officers, both of the United States and of the several states, shall be bound by oath or affirmation, to support this Constitution; but no religious test shall ever be required as a qualification to any office or public trust under the United States.

ARTICLE VII
Ratifying the Constitution

The ratification of the conventions of nine states, shall be sufficient for the establishment of this Constitution between the states so ratifying the same.

Done in convention by the unanimous consent of the states present the seventeenth day of September in the year of our Lord one thousand seven hundred and eighty-seven and of the independence of the United States of America the twelfth. In witness whereof we have hereunto subscribed our names.

Amendments to the Constitution

The first ten amendments, known as the Bill of Rights, were proposed on September 25, 1789. They were ratified, or accepted, on December 15, 1791. They were adopted because some states refused to approve the Constitution unless a Bill of Rights, protecting individuals from various unjust acts of government, was added.

Amendment 1

Freedom of religion, speech, and the press;
rights of assembly and petition

Amendment 2

Right to bear arms

Amendment 3

Housing of soldiers

Amendment 4

Search and arrest warrants

Amendment 5

Rights in criminal cases

Amendment 6

Rights to a fair trial

Amendment 7

Rights in civil cases

Amendment 8

Bails, fines, and punishments

Amendment 9

Rights retained by the people

Amendment 10

Powers retained by the states and the people

Amendment 11

Lawsuits against states

Amendment 12

Election of the President and Vice President

Amendment 13

Abolition of slavery

Amendment 14

Civil rights

Amendment 15

African-American suffrage

Amendment 16

Income taxes

Amendment 17

Direct election of senators

Amendment 18

Prohibition of liquor

Amendment 19

Women's suffrage

Amendment 20

Terms of the President and Congress

Amendment 21

Repeal of prohibition

Amendment 22

Presidential term limits

Amendment 23

Suffrage in the District of Columbia

Amendment 24

Poll taxes

Amendment 25

Presidential disability and succession

Amendment 26

Suffrage for eighteen-year-olds

Amendment 27

Congressional salaries

Chapter Notes

Chapter 1. Nat Turner's Rebellion

1. Ruth Wilson, *Our Blood and Tears: Black Freedom Fighters* (New York: G.P. Putnam's, 1972), p. 92.

2. Ibid., p. 90.

3. Stephen B. Oates, *The Fires of Jubilee: Nat Turner's Fierce Rebellion* (New York: New American Library, 1975), p. 61.

4. Wilson, p. 102.

5. Ibid.

6. Oates, p. 78.

7. Ibid., pp. 77–78.

8. Wilson, p. 106.

9. Harvey Wish, ed., "The Confessions of Nat Turner," in *Slavery in the South* (New York: Farrar, Straus & Giroux, 1969), pp. 16–17.

10. Wilson, p. 111.

11. Wish, p. 5.

12. Henrietta Buckmaster, *Let My People Go* (Columbia: University of South Carolina Press, 1992), p. 52.

13. Wish, p. 8.

14. Oates, p. 136.

Chapter 2. The Constitution and Slavery

1. Catherine Drinker Bowen, *Miracle at Philadelphia* (Boston: Little, Brown and Co., 1986), p. 28.

2. Richard B. Bernstein with Kym S. Rice, *Are We to Be a Nation? The Making of the Constitution* (Cambridge, Mass.: Harvard University Press, 1987), p. 152.

3. Ibid., p. 155.

4. Bowen, p. 201.

5. Ibid.

6. William Lee Miller, *Arguing About Slavery: The Great Battle in the United States Congress* (New York: Alfred A. Knopf, 1996), p. 14.

7. Bernstein, p. 5.

8. Richard B. Morris, *Witnesses at the Creation* (New York: Holt, Rinehart, and Winston, 1985), p. 207.

9. Ibid.

10. Bowen, p. 203.

11. Article I, Section 9, United States Constitution.

12. Article IV, Section 2, United States Constitution.

13. Bernstein, p. 177.

14. Ibid.

15. Miller, p. 19.

16. Ibid., pp. 19–20.

17. Richard B. Morris, *Witnesses at the Creation* (New York: Holt, Rinehart, and Winston, 1985), pp. 95, 98, 106.

18. Jim Haskins, *The Day Fort Sumter Was Fired On: A Photo History of the Civil War* (New York: Scholastic, 1995), p. 8.

Chapter 3. A Historical Overview of Slavery

1. Peter Kolchin, *American Slavery: 1619–1877* (New York: Hill & Wang, 1993), p. 11.

2. Ibid., p. 20.

3. Robert L. Liston, *Slavery in America: The Heritage of Slavery* (New York: McGraw-Hill, 1972), p. 37.

4. Kolchin, p. 22.

5. Bruce Levine, *Half Slave and Half Free: The Roots of Civil War* (New York: Hill and Wang, 1992), p. 29.

6. Solomon Northrup, *Twelve Years a Slave* (Baton Rouge: Louisiana State University Press, 1968), p. 126.

7. Levine, p. 30.

8. Editors of Time-Life Books, *Brother Against Brother: Time-Life Books History of the Civil War* (New York: Prentice Hall, 1990), p. 28.

9. Ibid., p. 25.

10. Bruno Leone, ed., *Slavery: Opposing Viewpoints* (San Diego, Calif.: Greenhaven Press, 1992), p. 80.

11. Ibid., p. 79.

12. John Hope Franklin, *From Slavery to Freedom: A History of Negro Americans* (New York: Alfred A. Knopf, 1980), p. 57.

13. Ibid., pp. 58–59.

14. Carol Ann Piggins, *A Multicultural Portrait of the Civil War* (New York: Marshall Cavendish, 1994), p. 26.

15. Judith Bentley, *Harriet Tubman* (New York: Franklin Watts, 1990), p. 17.

Chapter 4. The Seeds of Disunion and Civil War

1. Delia Ray, *A Nation Torn: The Story of How the Civil War Began* (New York: Lodestar/Dutton, 1990), p. 18.

2. Clarence L. Ver Steeg and Richard Hofstadter, *A People and a Nation* (New York: Harper & Row, 1971), p. 286.

3. Ray, pp. 19–20.

4. Ibid., pp. 24–25.

5. Ibid., p. 21.

6. Editors of Time-Life Books, *Brother Against Brother* (New York: Prentice Hall, 1990), p. 21.

7. Edwin C. Rozwenc, ed., *The Causes of the American Civil War* (Boston: D.C. Heath, 1961), p. 209.

8. Harvey Wish, ed., *Slavery in the South: First-Hand Accounts of the Ante-Bellum American Southland* (New York: Noonday/Farrar, Straus & Giroux, 1964), p. 271.

9. Rozwenc, p. 215.

10. T. Harry Williams, Richard N. Current, Frank Freidel, *A History of the United States*, vol. I (New York: Alfred A. Knopf, 1969), p. 316.

11. Ray, p. 36.

12. Samuel Eliot Morison, *The Oxford History of the American People*, vol. 2 (New York: New American Library, 1972), p. 139.

13. Ibid., p. 139.

14. Ray, p. 38.

15. Time-Life, p. 23.

Chapter 5. Harriet Tubman's Story

1. Charles L. Blockson, *The Underground Railroad* (New York: Prentice Hall Press, 1987), p. 118.

2. Judith Bentley, *Harriet Tubman* (New York: Franklin Watts, 1990), p. 39.

3. Blockson, p. 98.

4. Jim Haskins, *Get on Board: The Story of the Underground Railroad* (New York: Scholastic, 1993), p. 48.

5. Sarah Bradford, *Harriet Tubman, The Moses of Her People* (Secaucus, N.J.: Citadel Press, 1961), p. 33.

6. Raymond Bial, *The Underground Railroad* (Boston: Houghton Mifflin, 1995), p. 7.

7. Bentley, p. 58.

8. Ibid., p. 65.

Chapter 6. A Nation Torn—Slaves Are Freed

1. Editors of Time-Life Books, *Brother Against Brother* (New York: Prentice Hall, 1990), p. 57.

2. Ibid.

3. Ibid., p. 59; Timothy Levi Biel, *The Civil War* (San Diego, Calif.: Lucent Books, 1991), p. 51.

4. Biel, p. 16.

5. Ibid., p. 21.

6. Bruce Catton, *The Civil War* (Boston: Houghton Mifflin, 1988), p. 8.

7. Ibid., p. 8.

8. Delia Ray, *A Nation Torn: The Story of How the Civil War Began* (New York: Lodestar Books/Dutton, 1990), p. 48.

9. Catton, p. 10.

10. Ibid., p. 23.

11. James M. McPherson, *Battle Cry of Freedom* (New York: Oxford University Press, 1988), p. 332.

12. Funk & Wagnalls New Encyclopedia, vol. 6 (Chicago: Funk & Wagnalls, 1996), p. 340.

13. Joy Hakim, *War, Terrible War* (New York: Oxford University Press, 1994), Frontispiece.

14. McPherson, p. 497.

15. Samuel Eliot Morrison, *The Oxford History of the American People*, vol. 2 (New York: Oxford University Press, 1990), p. 30.

16. Biel, p. 93.

17. McPherson, p. 36.

18. William Lee Miller, *Arguing About Slavery: The Great Battle in the United States Congress* (New York: Alfred A. Knopf, 1996), p. 497.

19. Ibid., p. 93.

20. Ibid., p. 33.

21. McPherson, pp. 33–34.

22. Ibid., p. 86.

Chapter 7. Reconstruction and Its Aftermath

1. Patricia and Frederick McKissack, *The Civil Rights Movement in America from 1865 to the Present* (Chicago: Children's Press, 1987), p. 15.

2. Joy Hakim, *Reconstruction and Reform* (New York: Oxford University Press, 1994), p. 23.

3. John Anthony Scott, *The Story of America: A National Geographic Picture Atlas* (Washington, D.C.: The National Geographic Society, 1994), p. 182.

4. Grolier 1997 Multimedia Encyclopedia, "African-American History" (Danbury, Conn.: Interactive, 1996).

5. Scott, p. 186.

6. Hakim, p. 38.

7. Grolier, "African-American History."

8. McKissack, p. 49.

9. Ibid., pp. 50–51.

10. Scott, p. 193.

11. Grolier, "African-American History."

12. Ibid.

13. Hakim, pp. 48–49.

Chapter 8. Looking Toward the Future

1. Joy Hakim, *All the People* (New York: Oxford University Press, 1995), p. 77.

2. Sara Bullard, *Free At Last: A History of the Civil Rights Movement and Those Who Died in the Struggle* (New York: Oxford University Press, 1993), p. 19.

3. Ibid.

4. Hakim, p. 83.

5. Ibid., p. 85.

6. Grolier 1997 Multimedia Encyclopedia, "African-American History" (Danbury, Conn.: Grolier Interactive, 1996).

7. Michael Ryan, "How One Town Said 'No,'" *Parade* magazine, February 23, 1997, p. 5.

Further Reading

Bentley, Judith. *Harriet Tubman*. New York: Franklin Watts, 1990.

Bial, Raymond. *The Underground Railroad*. Boston: Houghton Mifflin, 1995.

Biel, Timothy Levi. *The Civil War*. San Diego, Calif.: Lucent Books, 1991.

Blockson, Charles L. *The Underground Railroad*. New York: Prentice Hall Press, 1987.

Bruno, Leone, ed. *Slavery: Opposing Viewpoints*. San Diego: Greenhaven Press, 1992.

Buckmaster, Henrietta. *Let My People Go: The Story of the Underground Railroad and the Growth of the Abolition Movement*. Columbia: University of South Carolina Press, 1992.

Celsi, Teresa. *Rosa Parks and the Montgomery Bus Boycott*. Brookfield, Conn.: The Millbrook Press, 1991.

Gillam, Scott. *Discrimination: Prejudice in Action*. Springfield, N.J.: Enslow Publishers, Inc., 1995.

Hakim, Joy. *All the People*. New York: Oxford University Press, 1995.

———. *Reconstruction and Reform*. New York: Oxford University Press, 1994.

———. *War, Terrible War*. New York: Oxford University Press, 1994.

Haskins, Jim. *Get On Board: The Story of the Underground Railroad*. New York: Scholastic, 1993.

Lucas, Eileen. *Civil Rights: The Long Struggle.* Springfield, N.J.: Enslow Publishers, Inc., 1996.

McKissack, Patricia and Frederick. *The Civil Rights Movement in America from 1865 to the Present.* Chicago: Children's Press, 1987.

Petry, Ann. *Harriet Tubman: Conductor on the Underground Railroad.* New York: Thomas Y. Crowell, 1955.

Piggins, Carol Ann. *A Multicultural Portrait of the Civil War.* New York: Marshall Cavendish, 1994.

Ray, Delia. *A Nation Torn: The Story of How the Civil War Began.* New York: Lodestar Books/Dutton, 1990.

Rochelle, Belinda. *Witnesses to Freedom: Young People Who Fought for Civil Rights.* New York: Lodestar/Dutton, 1993.

Sawyer, Kem Knapp. *The Underground Railroad in American History.* Springfield, N.J.: Enslow Publishers, Inc., 1997.

Scott, John Anthony. *The Story of America: A National Geographic Picture Atlas.* Washington, D.C.: The National Geographic Society, 1994.

Index